PROTECTING BUSINESS INFORMATION

AMERICAN SOCIETY FOR INDUSTRIAL SECURITY
1625 PRINCE STREET
ALEXANDRIA, VA 22314
(703) 519-6200

PROTECTING BUSINESS INFORMATION: A MANAGER'S GUIDE

James A. Schweitzer

Butterworth-Heinemann

Boston Oxford Melbourne Singapore Toronto Munich New Delhi Tokyo

Recognizing the importance of preserving what has been written, Butterworth-Heinemann prints its books on acid-free paper whenever possible.

Library of Congress Cataloging-in-Publication Data

Schweitzer, James A., 1929-
    Protecting business information : a manager's guide / James A. Schweitzer.
        p.   cm.
    Includes bibliographical references and index.
    ISBN 0-7506-9658-3 (alk. paper)

    1. Trade secrets. 2. Data protection. 3. Business intelligence. 4. Electronic data processing departments—Security measures. 5. Computer security. 6. Information resources management. I. Title.

HD38.7.S388 1995
658.4'72—dc20   95-9549
                                       CIP

British Library Cataloguing-in-Publication Data
A catalogue record for this book is available from the British Library.

The publisher offers discounts on bulk orders of this book.
For information, please write:

Manager of Special Sales
Butterworth-Heinemann
313 Washington Street
Newton, MA 02158-1626

10 9 8 7 6 5 4 3 2 1

Printed in the United States of America

Contents

Preface

*If one waits until a threat is manifest through a successful attack,
then significant damage can be done before an effective countermeasure can be developed and deployed. Therefore countermeasure
engineering must be based on speculation. Effort may be expended
in countering attacks that are never attempted. The need to specu-
late and to budget resources for countermeasures also implies a
need to understand what it is that should be protected, and why;
such understanding should drive the choice of a protection strategy
and countermeasures. This thinking should be captured in security
policies generated by management; poor security often reflects both
weak policy and inadequate forethought.*

National Research Council, *Computers at Risk*

In the 1990s:

- Information is critical to business success as fierce competition for market opportunities gives the advantage to companies with better technology and know-how.
- Corporate downsizing, the widespread use of temporary employees, and a dynamic
  employee population mean that loyalty is often to a technical specialty or a cause
  (perhaps oneself) rather than to the organization.
- The common use of computers and networks in all business activities makes information readily transferable and susceptible to misuse, sabotage, and fraud.

Therefore, business managers need to protect the information essential to the successful operation of their businesses.

This book is based on fifteen years of experience building and implementing information security programs for large, worldwide businesses. The presentation of the
material proceeds logically in a sequence intended for a managerial audience.

This book is for the security director who finds the responsibility for information
protection to be bewildering; for the information security manager who wishes to increase his or her understanding of a complex subject; and for the business manager who
must understand the reasoning and justification for investing in information protection.
For these readers, the index can be used to identify particular topics of interest. Many
case studies based on actual experience or on information provided by trusted sources
are offered as illustrations to support the methods proposed.

This book suggests practical ways to align an information security investment with business needs—that is, *to make information security a business process.* Effective protection of an intangible asset—such as information—requires a sense of purpose and dedication by almost all members of an organization. People are willing to perform difficult or inconvenient tasks when and if they are individually and collectively convinced that what they are doing is right or profitable for the company. An understanding of reasoning, purpose, and justification is the basis for commitment. Without this understanding, compliance may be perfunctory and may deteriorate over time. In the case of information protection, observance of the rules by a few or even by many employees is not sufficient. Effective security for a company's valuable and sensitive information requires consistent observance of the rules by all employees, at all times, and in all places where company business is transacted.

PART I

The Case for
Information Security

1

Background on Information Protection

This book will do the following:

- Persuade the reader that information protection is worthwhile and *necessary* in terms of business interests
- Illustrate the need for all employees to *commit* to the established company information protection regulations
- Explain how to establish effective information security as a business *process*

REASONS FOR INFORMATION PROTECTION

A business needs to establish and maintain a program for information protection for two reasons:

1. Information is an expensive, sensitive, and perishable resource. It is critical to competitive position and ultimately to the survival of the company. Rationally, the company must want to protect its information from loss of integrity, availability, and confidentiality and to preserve its authenticity and utility.[1]
2. Information represents a substantial investment. The strategies and plans (in other words, business information) that result from this investment are the keys to future market success.

The information value represented in business operations and product strategy plans and reports, which include technical, financial, and operational data, is probably equal to the value of the company less the value of physical assets. That is, if all information about how to run a business were to be lost, the residual value would probably be the selling price of plants and equipment. For most businesses, the true *competitive value* of the company is the value of its know-how, or information base.

INFORMATION IS A SENSITIVE RESOURCE

The very existence of a business eventually may depend on the ability of the company to create and deliver strategic products that are better than those of the competition. A competitor's acquisition of information concerning a company's plans or technical strategies may well provide the means for that competitor's spectacular leap ahead. In most cases, the purloined information provides data that save the competitor the time and cost of research necessary to make intelligent choices among technologies or marketing strategies. Two cases that demonstrate the critical importance of information, occurring over the past ten years, come to mind.

1. X Company was sued by C Company, because C alleged that X had created a "thicket of patents" that prevented C from successfully entering a line of business. The suit cost both companies tens of millions of dollars. Although the jury found for C, the judge overruled the decision to award damages. C abandoned the effort to enter a technology line of products. The profits of both companies were severely affected.
2. B Company discovered that H Company was buying strategic technical documents from B's employees. B successfully investigated these incidents and brought suit. H was restricted over a period of many years from taking a variety of actions bearing on H's principal business.

In both cases, although the circumstances were very different, technology-based companies were willing to spend large sums to protect information rights. In the first case, a competitor went to court to try, legally, to obtain strategic information. In the second case, the competitor tried to do the same thing illegally.

It is a fact that industrial espionage (the stealing of trade secrets) is fairly common, if seldom reported. The conclusion must be that much business information is wanted by competitors. Most competitors are ethical. But case records show that there is an active illegitimate market for valuable competitive information.

INFORMATION IS A PERISHABLE RESOURCE

Information may be nonrecoverable. Consider the traditional primary business resources: people, money, and materials. These resources can be lost through fire, flood, theft, fraud, sickness, death, or personal decisions to retire or work elsewhere. But these resources are reasonably recoverable. Very seldom has the loss of an employee, no matter how highly valued, or a plant or a supply of materials caused the demise of a successful business.

Once exposed or stolen, however, information cannot be recovered. Consider a family secret. Once it is told, it is no longer secret. One may bring suit for defamation or loss of privacy, but the resolution of the suit brings satisfaction, not a restoration of privacy. In the same way, business information is usually not recoverable. Exposed information about business or technical strategy is gone. It cannot be replaced, because its value is often in its exclusivity to its original owner. If everyone or even a few people know it, its value is diminished or destroyed.

The first goal in an information protection scheme is to prevent information from being exposed. However, if information is exposed or stolen (unfortunately, history says some of it will be), one needs to be prepared to prove ownership.

PROVING OWNERSHIP OF INFORMATION

Some information is claimed to be *proprietary* or *trade secret*. In general, proprietary information is that which has some commercial value and is closely held. All businesses have some information that is publicly known or available. An example is the street addresses of the facilities. It cannot be claimed that this information is proprietary. Similarly, some information is not publicly available but has no commercial value. An example might be an announcement of the time and place of a company picnic or sporting event. Such information cannot be claimed as proprietary. Figure 1–1 may help place the kinds of information in the proper categories.

HOW DO WE PROVE OWNERSHIP?

Proving ownership requires the following actions:

1. The company must have identified information it considers to have value. This identification process is called *classification*.
2. The company must have implemented procedures to identify (*mark* or *stamp*), process (*handle*, *store*), and generally protect valuable information in all forms (written, electronic, mental).

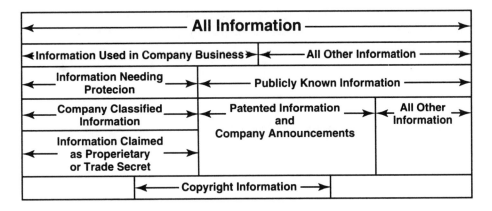

Figure 1–1   The information universe.

3. The company's employees must in the course of normal business operations consistently and routinely follow the rules established for protecting information.

In a case decided in 1980, a large electronics company lost rights to information because employees involved in a sensitive project were not instructed by their supervisor to follow the company's established information protection procedures.

PATENTS AND COPYRIGHTS

Patents and copyrights are legal measures used to protect proprietary information. Some copyrighted information and all patented information are public knowledge. Company classification of this type of information may not be appropriate. Questions about the use of patents or copyrights should be addressed to legal counsel.

CLASSIFICATION OF INFORMATION

Classification is the basic process for protecting information. One has to know which information is valuable in order to protect it properly. As with most valuables, one simply cannot protect everything. Doing so would be expensive and impractical and may compromise claims of proprietary rights.

The goal of an information protection effort is to prevent exposure, theft, improper modification, or destruction of information. If the information is properly classified, and if all employees and other trusted people follow the agreed-upon rules for access, handling, and storage of the information, the company will succeed in protecting this valuable resource. Information classification processes are discussed in detail in chapter 5.

SUMMARY

Management is responsible for protecting business assets. Information is a primary and expensive asset. Protection of this asset is a complex, dynamic activity that requires considerable effort.

NOTES

1. Donn B. Parker, *ISP News*, May/June 1991.

2

The Management Issue: Why Bother with Information Security?

Information security. The methods, procedures, and processes necessary to prevent unauthorized disclosure, modification, or destruction of information, or the loss of proprietary rights thereto. Applies to all information forms: paper, microforms, photographs, transparencies, magnetic (electronic), and human memory.

> Lawyers are increasingly taking the position that the vulnerabilities and safeguards relating to information have become sufficiently well known to assume that information protection now falls under the "ordinary care" responsibilities of company directors. If [this position is] upheld by courts, directors could find themselves liable for breach of information trust, should confidential information be disclosed through management carelessness or lack of effective security measures.[1]

"I've never seen such paranoia!" This comment came from a new college graduate just starting his first job as a computer programmer. He had just read the security requirements for applications to be run in the data centers of a large American business.

This skeptical newcomer was not by himself in viewing security as an unreasonable, unnecessary, and tedious requirement. Most people do not like to consider unpleasant prospects. Although we all know about street crime, burglaries, automobile theft, and so forth as aspects of modern life, we try not to think about them. As a result, people usually install home security systems after the burglars have done their work and the family's valuables are gone. Similarly, in spite of massive evidence that shows the benefits of using them, many are still reluctant to fasten automobile seat belts.

Humans fear recognizing risk, because doing so admits to an unhappy side of life. Business managers are no different. Like aircraft accidents, most of the security incidents reported in print and broadcast news are seen to affect "someone else."

An additional factor affects our reluctance to accept threats to information security: Many information espionage or damage cases are kept under wraps. Most businesses (and governments) are unwilling to make public their information security breaches. For cogent or sometimes questionable reasons, managers prefer to keep security problems private. They frequently choose not to prosecute the perpetrator even when he or she is known, because of the unfavorable publicity attendant on most such cases.

The unknowing employee often sees information security as bureaucratic non-sense imposed by unsmiling security professionals whose demeanor may reflect a military or police background.

PRACTICAL BUSINESS JUDGMENT

Information security is a rational response to serious economic and competitive matters. Information is among the most critical, expensive business resources. In his landmark book *Megatrends*, John Naisbitt tells us that the strategic and most important business resource is information.[2] Having sole possession of unique or innovative pieces of information can assure business success and profitability. On the other hand, losing information advantage can mean loss of market, risk of a lawsuit, or perhaps even business failure.

Case

In 1990, three Argentine citizens were sentenced in U.S. District Court for theft of information and blackmail. The three stole secret plans from E.I. DuPont, amounting to more than 1300 printed pages, and then tried to blackmail the company. Two of the men were DuPont employees.[3]

Information is a critical business resource. It deserves a carefully designed protection effort for the following reasons:

- Product information (e.g., technology) represents a competitive advantage.
- Market information provides strategic knowledge necessary for business success.
- Information about employees and their skills and placement may offer valuable insight to competitors.
- Business plans are important and must be kept confidential to protect advantages that may be gained from unique technological or market information.
- Financial data must, in many cases, be kept confidential because of requirements of law. Common sense dictates that some financial information be held within the company.
- The expense of developing, delivering, and using information (information costs) is significant. Any expensive resource should be properly protected.
- Information, alone among all business assets, may be irreplaceable.

Let's discuss each of these reasons for investment in information security.

Product Design and Manufacturing Know-how

Product design and manufacturing know-how represent the most important competitive advantage in business today. Companies often seize and hold market dominance on the basis of a unique capability to produce "better or cheaper widgets." Competitors strive to produce similar products with what are, they hope, at least perceived advantages. A company in a technology-rich industry finds itself continually fighting for an information advantage. That is, it recognizes that it must repeatedly come up with innovative methods and ideas that are kept confidential until the latest possible moment. Few industries today are isolated from the demand to generate better competitive information that in some way offers at least a temporary competitive advantage.

High-technology industries provide easily understood illustrations of the importance and costs of information. As technological research has accelerated, often as a result of government-sponsored defense spending, the life cycle of a product has been compressed to a relatively small time frame. When a new product is introduced, competitors buy the product and immediately begin work on a "better" replacement.

The original investment in research and engineering represents the information advantage, the *market edge*. If the work to develop a competing product can be shortened by obtaining information (perhaps illicitly) about the originator's research and engineering decisions, the imitator has an immediate advantage. In some cases, the time during which the original product has an innovation-based advantage can be reduced to almost nothing. The development costs that usually are amortized may be partially or altogether avoided. Product differentiators that are the result of stolen information may allow pricing that drives the original developer from the market.

Market Intelligence Data

Market intelligence data, especially if more correct or better than that obtained by others, can be an important advantage. The advantage exists only as long as the entrepreneurial business is able to keep secret the unique market information and the plans for the use of that information (*marketing strategies*). Cases involving businesses that failed because management did not perceive the market properly are common. American railroads came close to failure because they saw their business as "railroad" rather than "transportation" and thus long neglected ideas such as Trailer Train.

The business of ferreting out information about competitors' plans is a thriving industry. Organizations such as Washington Researchers provide data and offer schools on competitive information gathering. Industrial espionage is not uncommon. In their book *Industrial Espionage,* Bottom and Gallati say,"The entire range of employees from top executive down to the mail carrier or the cleaning staff are potential (industrial) spies given the right price."[4]

Companies that are downsizing, are in decline, or are in temporary trouble are most likely to experience a loss of employee loyalty. Workers fearful of losing their jobs may see information provided in trust as an opportunity to prepare for the worst.

> Having an understanding of the intentions of our competitors is absolutely essential to our prevailing. We are at war, and to win battles we have to have the information to prepare strategic and tactical responses to the actions of our competitors. You can't be satisfied with where your competitor is now or where he has just been. You've got to know where he is going.[5]

Personal Information

Personal information, by its nature, requires that the holder ensure its confidentiality. Examples of sources of information in this category are personnel records, health and insurance records, employee performance appraisals, and plans for transfer or separation of key managers. Many jurisdictions require special government approvals for and stipulate rigorous control over personal information of any kind.

Privacy is a key issue in the 1990s. Abuses of information by governments and other mass collectors of personal data have resulted in a strong movement for privacy and the enactment of various laws to that end. Security for such information may be a matter not only of ethical considerations but also of financial self-interest, since severe penalties may be incurred.

Unannounced Strategic Business Plans and Decisions

Unannounced strategic business plans and decisions, including the sale or purchase of real property, investment in other companies, divestment of subsidiaries, and similar information, should be protected as a matter of simple business prudence. The secrecy of such plans may relate directly to their success. Unauthorized exposure of plans to buy property or businesses usually causes the price of such activity to increase precipitously.

Financial Information

Financial information may be covered by disclosure laws that mandate the protection of certain types of information, such as unannounced financial results, to prevent abuses in the equities markets. As noted with regard to privacy, management should recognize financial as well as ethical motivation in protecting unannounced financial data.

The Cost of Information

Information costs money. Although managers often act as if they believe information is free, most intuitively know that information represents an investment. Titles such as vice president for information management reflect increasing awareness of information costs. As a practical matter, all business managers should have an interest in protecting the company's information investment. Information that has become public or has been exposed (perhaps clandestinely to competitors) may lose all its value, just as a business may suffer a loss when products or raw materials are stolen or destroyed in a fire.

Some computer companies have estimated that the real cost of developing, processing, and delivering information necessary to business success may be as much as 5 percent to 7 percent of revenues. These startling cost estimates suggest that in modern businesses, many heavily oriented toward service activities, most employees are *knowledge workers*. They work with information rather than, for example, with materials (production workers) or natural resources (miners). Knowledge workers include managers, scientists, engineers, secretaries, and others. Most of these people use computers as a primary tool. Their principal task is generating and delivering information, much of which has sufficient value and importance to justify protection.

Inability to Replace Information

Information may be irreplaceable. People, facilities, raw materials, and finished products can be replaced, at a cost. This may not be true of information. Consider a case in which a secret process is divulged publicly in a trade magazine. The original owner may bring a lawsuit against those responsible for the exposure. Even if the suit is successful, the result may be an award far from the equivalent of the business potential that results from the secret process. Consider the damage to the reputation of a company known for its consideration of workers when an employee leaks a memo to a newspaper. The memo, intended for only a few top executives, discusses planned layoffs. There is no way to recover a secret!

In one case, some employees of a computer company in Texas started a competitive business. Although the original company prevailed after lengthy court trials, the market opportunity for the product in question had disappeared and the original investment was wasted. The value of unique and secret competitive data could not be recovered.

TAKING A POSITION

Senior business management may choose to ignore information security. When this occurs, it is usually because the people involved do not comprehend the nature of the information resource. Some common fallacious views are as follows:

"We don't have any information that is really valuable."

"Our computers are protected."

"This is not a big company and we all know what needs to be done."

"Information security is simple common sense. Just protect it."

DEFINING THE SUBJECT

Information is an intangible asset. It occurs in three forms: *written*, *electronic*, and *mental*. To protect the information resource, equivalent security must be provided for all three forms. Managers tend to think about information security as being the same as computer security. Emphasis on protection of the electronic form of information often leads to a faulty vision of what is required to protect all information. Many managers continue to believe that information security is the responsibility of the information system manager. This posture is an incorrect assumption that the most important risk to information is through computers when in fact the worst threats are loose talk and careless handling and copying of pieces of paper.

Case

A large industrial company in Connecticut attempted to establish an information security process through the information systems department. Eventually, all of the data center computers were secured, and computer-generated reports were marked with company information classifications. The effort foundered because reports produced on office word-processing systems were not marked. Perceptive employees recognized the double standard as a way out of the inconveniences attendant to proper security.[6]

To ensure an effective program, one that protects information in all appropriate forms, managers must view information protection as one of the basic security functions, rather than as a part of information systems or administration.

The information security responsibilities of a company belong to the company security director, who is responsible for protecting all business assets. As is the case with manufacturing or engineering facilities or processes that require security, technical security requirements may have to be handled by others (e.g., putting access-control software into effect may require a software programmer, but he or she acts as an agent of the security manager). The information security program is part of the overall company security effort.

MANAGEMENT CONSIDERATION OF RISKS

Having a reasonable conception of the threats to business information is important. A senior manager from a grocery company once made the statement, "I don't think we have any information that needs protection." But the manager changed his mind when asked, "How would you feel if you discovered a stranger going through your office files?"

The greatest risks come from a company's own employees, those authorized to access, retrieve, modify, move, or display information. Remember we are talking about *all three forms* of information: mental, paper, electronic. An employee may discover in the course of an authorized job process that unintended access to information or inventive manipulation is possible. This threat may involve computer systems or paper-based systems.

A well-known threat is the *computer hacker*, a term that has become generalized to include anyone who may use computer access to information that may be observed, stolen, transferred, or modified while in electronic form. Although the specter of the distant, unknown genius who breaks through security to access secret data is a common worry, in reality "computer crime" cases usually involve trusted employees. These people may have personal problems or job dissatisfaction, and they see a possible solution when they discover a flaw in security or control systems.

The usual means of threat realization is the plain paper copier. By far the most common industrial espionage methods involve surreptitious removal of papers. Those paying large sums of money for information prefer to see what they are buying before making payment. All the espionage cases reported to date by the United States Defense Investigative Service involve transfer of paper. Other threats may involve careless exposure or intentional unauthorized use of information retained in memory.

Case

In a case near Rochester, New York, an engineer drew ideas for a critical machinery component on a tablecloth in a restaurant during lunch. Another customer, seeking that information for a competitor, bought the tablecloth from the restaurant owner.

A cornucopia of information for competitors is usually the bar or restaurant where the people involved in critical, leading-edge work meet to unwind after hours. Conversations almost always turn to business matters, and as a few drinks are consumed tongues loosen. Most information security failures result from gross carelessness or ignorance on the part of trusted people.

There are computer hackers, but in almost every case they are able to do what they do because of negligence or carelessness on the part of employees.

Case

In one notable case, a hacker placed a long-distance telephone call to a well-known company's data center. In the cold call the hacker persuaded the computer operator to load a tape. The hacker copied the tape and stored it. The tape contained extremely valuable licensing materials, which were later recovered during a criminal investigation.

Understanding the threats is important to having the commitment necessary to achieve acceptable information security. But security is expensive. It is therefore important that senior management understand why the effort is necessary and then take a strong, correctly oriented position on information security.

FORMING A RISK ACCEPTANCE POSTURE

Information security always poses a choice. Any information security process has three desirable characteristics: convenience, economy, and appropriate protection. In any given circumstance the business manager can have only two of the three characteristics, as the following shows:

- An information security process that is convenient to use and that provides appropriate protection is expensive. A process that is economical and convenient to use provides little security.
- A system (manual or electronic) that provides adequate security but is not expensive is difficult and inconvenient for the users.
- A process that is inexpensive and easy to use does not offer effective protection. Figure 2—1 illustrates this situation.

The first step to information security is the development of a risk acceptance posture. In other words, how much risk is management willing to take? After all, business itself is a matter of taking risks.

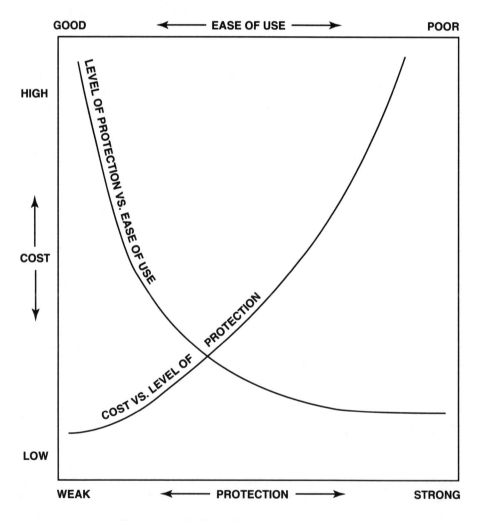

Figure 2–1   Problem of protection cost versus risk.

INFORMATION SECURITY IS A BUSINESS DECISION

Managers should not be satisfied with advice from security managers that offers no alternatives to traditional "protection of assets" approaches. Options to security measures include the transfer of risk to others through insurance policies, acceptance of carefully defined risks as a cost of doing business, and the selection of alternative information protection methods (manual or automated). The following are risk management alternatives:

- Avoidance (don't do)
- Evasion (do alternative)
- Assumption (accept risk as a cost of business)
- Hedging (use backup or replacement plan)
- Reduction (execute security precautions)
- Transference (buy insurance policy)

The work required to allow a management decision on information risk acceptance is described in subsequent chapters. It suffices here to say that such a decision must be based on an evaluation (or *classification*) of the information elements of the business to identify the various levels of protection required. This process should tell management exactly what needs to be safeguarded, based on *information values* or *sensitivities*. Properly designed, effective, and economical security measures can be designed only after the business has determined information values. Policy developed from this awareness of the value of information can provide protection that expresses management's risk acceptance position.

SUMMARY

Information is probably the most critical business resource. Providing suitable protection is a complex matter. An effective protection scheme flows from an identification of information values and a recognition of the risks management is willing to accept.

NOTES

1. Paraphrased from Peter Marx, *Infoworld*, August 16, 1986, and J.J. BloomBecker, *Datamation*, October 15, 1989.
2. John Naisbitt, *Megatrends* (New York: Warner Books, 1982), 15.
3. United Press International, March 7, 1990
4. Norman Bottom and Robert Gallati, *Industrial Espionage* (Boston: Butterworth, 1984), 35.
5. Robert Hudson, manager of Strategic Information, Eastman Kodak Company; *Rochester Business Journal*, October 16–22, 1989.
6. Paraphrased from Donn B. Parker, *ISSA Access*, January–March 1990.

3

Information Threats and Vulnerabilities

Some true stories illustrate the information threats and vulnerabilities described in this chapter.

Case

Some teenage boys, using a home computer and modem, connected with a business computer by using a telephone number from the phone book. When they received a greeting screen, they used the HELP command to determine various actions, which eventually led to their taking control. They were able to grant privileges and establish accounts. The company that owned the computer had to terminate business for a weekend to reestablish security.

Case

A supervisor helped a discharged employee carry boxes to his car. Later, the former employee tried to sell the contents of the boxes, which were plans for a new product, back to the company.

DEFINITIONS

Threat. A threat is a probable action that may compromise the integrity, privacy, or reliability of an information set. Threats usually take advantage of vulnerabilities.

Vulnerability. A vulnerability is a weakness or hole in security against threats.

Table 3–1 illustrates and contrasts some of the characteristics of information threats and vulnerabilities.

Modern piracy is being practiced in laboratories, production plants, and in classrooms by ordinary managers, workers, and students who appropriate for their own use the ideas or inventions belonging to others or to their employers. The United States government estimates that information thieves cost United States businesses $60–100 billion each year. While the tradition of intellectual property comes down to us from the times of Plato and Aristotle, current trends

Table 3–1   Threats and Vulnerabilities

	Threat	*Vulnerability*
Source		
	Internal or external	Internal
Cause		
	Discontent	Ignorance
	Technical curiosity	Technical flaws or errors
	Greed	Carelessness
	Aggression	

to industrial espionage and information theft threaten the system of reward for innovation, which has driven improvements in the standard of living for many.[1]

In the cases presented, threats came from outside (the teenagers and the hacker) and inside (the discharged employee). The threats were motivated by technical curiosity (teenagers), greed (hacker), and discontent, aggression, and greed (former employee).

The vulnerabilities in the cases involve internal problems. The teenagers succeeded because the computer owner had failed to install practical, technical security measures. The hacker obtained the file because the data center employee was ignorant and because sufficient security measures were missing. The former employee was able to steal the papers because his supervisor was ignorant or careless.

TYPES OF THREATS

Information threats are of two types. The first is a threat against the integrity, privacy, or reliability of the information.

> *Integrity* means that the information is as accurate and timely as the user expects it to be.

> *Privacy* means that the information is exposed only to those so authorized by the information owner.

> *Reliability* means that the information is delivered or presented when and where needed.

Integrity, privacy, and reliability are characteristics of quality information in any form—mental, electronic, or written.

The second type of threat involves damage to the information infrastructure, that is, damage to computers, networks, file cabinets, safes, storage areas, and other facilities.

SOURCES OF THREATS

Insider Threats

Employee (insider) threats to information constitute the most severe danger to business data. Employees and other authorized insiders are a threat to information. This threat may be realized because of carelessness, incompetence, or ignorance; purposeful actions due to discontent or curiosity; or personal needs such as financial problems.

A 1989 study conducted by the National Center for Computer Crime Data reported the following:[2]

- Employee revenge is a leading cause of breaches of computer security.
- Only 27 percent of employees in large companies were aware of their company's ethics code.
- The average reported loss due to computer abuse was $109,000, 965 staff hours, or 26 computer hours. (These data are probably skewed to the high end of the actual range because most incidents are not reported.)
- Most computer-related crimes were committed by employees (26 percent), students (26 percent), and unemployed people or previously convicted criminals (19 percent).

What about Errors?   Contrary to the statements made by many security experts, employee errors in the course of authorized, routine business operations are not a security matter. Normal human error is a supervisory and training issue. Although many security officials identify human error in routine business as a security threat, one only needs consider whether the company security director is held responsible for secretarial, administrative, or manufacturing errors in typing, recording, assembly, packing, addressing, or shipping. Obviously not. Some employee errors, however, may directly affect security and these are a matter for concern.

Case

An American businessman paid $45 for some "junk" computer equipment, only to find out later that sensitive government files concerning criminal investigations had not been properly erased from the computer's disks. When the U.S. government requested the return of those disks, the purchaser said he was unable to identify the particular computer from among many similar machines in his stock. Now the government is suing for return. The buyer said, "I am being punished for the inefficiency of the government."[3]

Outsider Threats

Outsider threats to date mostly involve stealing pieces of paper. Professional industrial spies want to know what they are buying, and they do not trust floppy disks. Industrial spies who do the most damage do not want to be recognized or discovered. This may be the reason that professional attacks on the information infrastructure are rare. Spies prefer to get away with the information and disappear without notice.

A large group of outsiders represents an amateur threat; these are the so-called computer hackers. Some people see computer access as a means to express social discontent. Others have technical curiosity, which may lead to mischievous behavior. Still others may see opportunity for profit in finding weaknesses by chance encounter.

Case

The mother of a 12-year-old boy charged as a computer hacker felt relieved that the child stayed in his room four or five hours a night playing with his computer. "He didn't bother me," she said, "He sat there on his computer. Well, I figured, computers—that's the thing of the day." While "sitting there," the boy accessed TRW Credit Corporation computers and posted credit card data to a number of computer bulletin board systems. The result was massive fraud. The boy reportedly excels in mathematics and geography.[4]

The computer threat to information from outsiders is increasing as computer systems become ever more interconnected, and as standards are put in place that eliminate protocol differences that have heretofore prevented easy interconnection. The computer networks, in fact, will soon be just like the telephone networks. A common query is, how would you like to have a bell in your house that anyone in the world could ring? You do! It's called the telephone.

The United States National Research Council, in a 1991 report entitled *Computers at Risk*,[5] identified a number of trends that indicate society is at a discontinuity, a position where we may no longer assume that we can rely on history as a guide. These trends are as follows:

- A proliferation of networks and embedded systems that are changing the installed base of computers and applications
- The integration of computers as an integral part of business so that computer risks are inherent
- Widespread use of databases that contain sensitive personal information
- Increasing use of computers in critical applications in which society must trust system reliability
- An increasingly common capability on the part of citizens to use and abuse computer systems
- An unstable political environment, in which people may view computer systems as a means to make a political statement

Outsiders may threaten the information infrastructure (as did the teenagers in the case at the beginning of this chapter) by overloading resources or interfering with operation. Often, outsiders (hackers) who are only curious may browse through company files; the matter turns serious if they discover opportunities for profit. An aggressive hacker may intend to interfere or steal, because of greed, aggression, or perhaps a desire for anarchy.

Hackers are not necessarily teenagers. In a story on May 28, 1990, *Middlesex News* (Massachusetts) presented details about hackers ("Who Uses Computer Bulletin Boards?"):

- Most are older than 25 years.
- One-third earn more than $35,000 a year.
- Thirty-eight percent have conservative political beliefs.
- Forty-four percent say use of bulletin board systems is job-related.
- Ninety-four percent are men.

Case

Nicholas Whiteley, the first computer hacker to be sentenced by courts in the United Kingdom, accessed several university computers in the U.K. from the Joint Academic Network (called "Janet"). He used friendly user commands such as HELP and INFO to figure out how to get privileges, and was able to guess some passwords and system IDs. He printed out messages at several universities and so overloaded the Hull University computer that the machine had to be taken out of service. Whiteley is quoted "I only wanted to learn about communications and security. I had read books that [said that] universities did not mind. They used a set-up without passwords so that anyone could drop in."[6]

THE VARIETY OF THREATS AND VULNERABILITIES

There is an almost limitless variety of threats to information. Industrial espionage professionals are becoming better trained and more inventive as the competitive search for profits, fueled by a scarcity of information resources with potential, intensifies. The list of ways to attack computers and networks grows daily as new technologies and new ideas pour out of the vast computing industry, universities, and millions (billions?) of everyday computer users.

Many clever ideas are delivered by way of the many computer bulletin board systems. Bulletin board systems involve private individuals or groups who operate, usually from home, one or more computers connected to telephone or data networks. Some bulletin boards are licit, and the users are interested only in learning and communicating. Other bulletin boards are clearly criminal. Most, however, operate in an ill-defined area in which ideas on all subjects are exchanged, explored, and developed.

Many businesses are now using electronic data interchange (EDI). EDI involves the direct computer-to-computer communication of common business documents such as purchase orders, bills of lading, invoices, and checks. Vulnerabilities in EDI include misdirected or diverted orders or payments, unauthorized payments, compromise of sensitive information, and other improper or unauthorized activities performed through the use of the networks. As currently conceived, EDI contains few robust security measures. Typical identification processes are applied, and encryption or other validity checking measures may be available. Often, however, a business user of EDI is concerned only with efficiency of transactions and does not consider security.

The portable or cellular telephone is a very serious vulnerability. The proliferation of this equipment and the availability of cheap, efficient eavesdropping equipment mean that no one can assume that conversations using portable telephones are private. In January 1990, the magazine *Monitoring Times* offered thirteen different scanner products capable of monitoring cellular telephones. And a book, *Tune in on Telephone Calls,* by Tom Knietel explains how to do it. Television channels 80 through 83 also offer an easy way to eavesdrop; these channels use the same frequencies as cellular phones.[7]

The complexity of computing sometimes results in security breaches.

Case

A bank offered credit to a "person" whose supposed name was a result of a computer garble. A company name, Friedman, Weddington and Hansen was abbreviated during processing and showed on the computer record as "Friedman, Wedd et al." This was further convoluted in the creation of a mailing list to Etalfried Wedd. This fictitious entity was then offered a preapproved loan based on a "good credit record."[8]

PHYSICAL THREATS AND VULNERABILITIES

Physical threats to information include fire, water, theft of papers or media, bombings, power failure, acts of God, careless handling, unauthorized destruction, and improper waste management.

In the United States, fire is clearly a most serious risk to information availability. Data center fires have been especially traumatic. In several cases reported over the past twenty years, a fire in another part of a building resulted in tons of water damaging computers and data media. Fire safety and preparedness is a basic information security requirement. Storage of back-up documents and media in proper containers or better yet in distant, secured facilities is essential.

Common theft, sometimes helped by the availability of plain paper copiers, is also a serious and present threat to information privacy and confidentiality. Other than the electronic attacks, which threaten information integrity or reliability, the theft of papers or copies of papers continues to be the primary method used to deliver business information to unauthorized parties.

Both information security technologists and the mass media's reporting of computer crimes have convinced many managers that the most vulnerable form of information is that which is stored electronically and sent through communications lines. This is not true, however, according to continuing research on computer abuse and interviews with perpetrators and victims. The most vulnerable form of information is still that which is spoken, followed by printed and displayed information. Then comes information stored on removable media, in computers, and finally, in communications lines and switches.[9]

Case

An executive wrote a memo about business plans and sent it to another manager on the company network. The originator failed to mark the document with the appropriate company classification. The recipient's secretary, following long-standing procedure, forwarded the electronic note to the departmental staff. Several staff members made further distributions. Somewhere in all this passing of information, a copy that was printed found its way to a national newspaper, which printed an embarrassing story based on the memo. The vulnerabilities were the employees' ignorance or carelessness. The threat of information exposure was realized when an insider made an unauthorized copy and delivered it to an outsider.

The first mishandling of information was by the originator; his error compounded later ignorance or carelessness by many employees. The actual theft of information was perpetrated by the person who removed the printed copy of the note from the premises.

Wastebaskets, industrial waste containers, garbage dumps, and similar depositories for unwanted business paper are gold mines for industrial spies and computer hackers. Companies may spend thousands of dollars on computer security software to protect sensitive information and then throw papers that contain the same information into waste systems that provide no information protection. Inventive computer hackers and other miscreants sort through waste containers to find potentially valuable materials and often come up with access procedures and passwords.

Case

XYZ Company opened a new office building and contracted with a hauler to take away paper refuse. After a time, the hauler asked why there was seldom any paper to be removed. Parties unknown had been picking up the waste paper.

Case

In southern California, a man sorted though trash outside a telephone office and removed instructions on how to access and modify the company's switching computers. As a result, he was able to penetrate the company's computers, to change service levels, and to provide free telephone calls for himself and others.

In both these cases, the original information owner seems to have regarded information as valueless. This state of mind—not uncommon—is a vulnerability. Employee awareness and willingness to follow information protection procedures are vital in the handling of waste.

We can stipulate the following rule:

All company classified materials in any form must be destroyed beyond recovery by burning or pulverization at the end of the useful life of the material.

ELECTRONIC THREATS AND VULNERABILITIES

Both employees and outsiders can threaten electronic information. The threats may result in violation of the integrity, privacy, or reliability of the information when a vulnerability so allows. There are two types of electronic threats—direct and indirect.

Direct threats include the following:

Purposeful unauthorized penetration of computer systems and files that occurs with or without an attack on a security mechanism

Opportunistic unauthorized actions against computers and their data files—perhaps initiated by chance discovery of a flaw—that occur during authorized activities. This threat is from insiders.

Indirect threats involve the introduction of harmful agents through the unwitting actions of employees or by means of mischievous or malicious actions by outsiders.

Direct Threats

Purposeful Unauthorized Penetrations   Purposeful unauthorized penetrations occur when an outsider attempts to connect with computers in which he or she has no rights. The attempts may be made from a home computer, from work, or from a university laboratory. The connection may be made from a network on which the penetrator has rights and which is shared by the target computer. Or the attack may be started with a test of a telephone number—with an autodialer—or by use of forcible methods that involve trying of thousands of passwords.

Good security, properly implemented, stops most of these attempts before a connection is made with computer operating systems or information. Unfortunately, thousands of computers are not protected, and in some cases, are operated with a cavalier and arrogant attitude, which invites successful attack.

Case

High school students tested various telephone numbers and found one that allowed them to connect their school computer to a computer used by a city hospital. The students were able to change data files and to cause widespread confusion. The hospital had simply not considered security when the system was installed.

Opportunistic Unauthorized Threats   Opportunistic unauthorized threats to information occur because there are flaws in control processes or because system designers (of both electronic and manual systems) failed to recognize or address possible control weaknesses. Some of these faults may be in the computer operating system. Others may involve simple paper handling.

Case

A large company used a terminal in its headquarters to direct large cash transfers among depository banks and suppliers. The documents that authorized the transfers were signed by an officer before the transfer instructions were issued, but no one in authority ever looked at the reports of transfer provided by the bank. These were merely filed away as audit documents. An employee transferred funds to an account in a bank in another time zone just before close of business at corporate headquarters but well before the end of the day at the receiving bank. The money was withdrawn later that day. The transaction was not noticed until the end of the week.

Indirect Threats

Indirect, or passive, threats include various software constructions that may cause unexpected or unwanted actions, often hidden. These threats are passive because they often require action on the part of ignorant or unwitting users to trigger the attack. If an attempt to use any of these threats is successful, it is so because, at least to some degree, the people involved have not been properly trained or made aware of the potential for damage. Although computer security is important, most threats to information are realized because of procedural or administrative failures. The threats include the following.

Virus   So-called *virus* programs are sets of software instructions that have an *appending* characteristic. When the virus instruction set is exposed to other programs, it performs a process that adds the virus to the instruction set of the programs. The virus may carry with it instructions that may be neutral, helpful, or harmful.

A virus could be prepared that would issue a "Good Day!" greeting each time a program is run. A virus might be used to introduce useful functions in all programs run in a location. Most often, a virus carries instructions that create mischief or cause damage or prevent useful computing operations. Because the appending instruction requires direct contact between the virus and a target program, viruses cannot be spread without some cooperation by the victim. The infected program must be loaded and run.

The popularity of games and utility programs for microcomputers and the prevalence of software piracy—copying software without license from the owner—has provided the direct contact needed to spread a virus. Many programs in so-called freeware libraries contain virus software. When employees bring computer games and other programs into the workplace from home, a severe threat arises.

Worm   A *worm* program finds network address lists and then mails itself to those addresses. A very early worm program was written about 1975 at the Xerox Palo Alto Research Center. It was intended to correct a common fault in many computers attached to a network. More recently a demonstration worm created by a student at Cornell University went through the Research Internet and caused massive computer failures. This worm was intended to be only a demonstration of how such a program could replicate itself. Unfortunately, an error in the programming created a monster. Like a virus, a worm can be helpful, neutral, or harmful and can carry with it many of the following software programs.

Trojan Horse   A *Trojan horse* is a software program that appears to offer some benefit, service, or entertainment. However, given certain conditions such as user actions, date or time, or loading of files, a secret function is activated. A favorite Trojan horse involves erasure of the pointers (or formatting) for data files on a hard disk, effectively destroying a user's files. To be run successfully, a Trojan Horse requires unwitting assistance from the computer user.

Trapdoor   A *trapdoor* is computer program code that allows undetected entry into supposedly secure areas of a computer system. Such code may be provided by system builders to allow quick repair of faults. In some cases it may be surreptitiously created. Morrie Gasser pointed out that "a trap door is useful only in software that runs with privileges that the penetrator does not otherwise have . . . for that reason we usually think of trap doors in operating systems and not in applications."[10] Careful review of programs by several people is a safeguard. It is unrealistic, however, to believe that most operating systems can be thoroughly checked. The *kernel* operating system is an effort to make the security control portion of the system small enough that a reliability check can be performed.

Salami or Diddler   *Salami* or *diddler* programs are hidden in applications. They institute processes that are contrary to the intent of the program's sponsor. The salami program is usually used for fraud. It is used to round numbers to collect money in very small increments from large numbers of computations and to transfer these overages to an unauthorized file. The diddler program is used to make subtle changes in information that allow illicit activities such as kiting or unauthorized transfers of funds among accounts to cover shortages.

   If an attempt to use any of these threats is successful, it is so because, at least to some degree, the people involved have not been properly trained or made aware of the potential for damages. Although computer security is important, most often information threats are realized because of procedural or administrative failures.

Case

A manufacturer of industrial equipment discovered that products sent to a customer did not perform properly. Problem analysis showed that the microcomputers embedded in the products had been infected with a virus. An investigation revealed that an employee had brought a computer game from home and had run it on a computer that was also used for developmental work on software that supported product functions. The manufacturer had failed to ensure a clean environment for critical work.

VULNERABILITIES

Insider Threats

Employee or insider threats succeed most often because of vulnerabilities in the control process provided to business operations. For example, can the company do the following?

* Prove who used the computer to perform an action
* Identify the person who packed or shipped materials
* Identify who was provided with a copy of a sensitive document
* Limit access to information and the possible actions taken (read, modify, delete, copy) to those specifically authorized by the information owner

Although technical safeguards such as computer (logical) access controls are helpful in limiting vulnerabilities, simple measures such as effective supervision and good training are the bases for control. Vulnerabilities result from management failure to install security and control measures and to properly train and supervise employees.

Most companies employ highly skilled computer experts, who are necessary to maintain operating system software or to do troubleshooting. These people often love computing for its own sake. The term *hacker* originally meant someone who was inventive in using computers. Today, the term has a pejorative meaning that implies mischievous intent.

Vulnerabilities that involve technical expertise occur when controls are not provided. Good management control means that the company knows what these technical experts are doing. For example, modifications to operating system software, security controls, and application programs should be reviewed by management. It may be wise to motivate the experts with creative computing opportunities outside the realm of business operational computing.

Outsider Vulnerabilities

Vulnerabilities to attacks from outside almost always originate in technical or procedural shortcomings. These can be manual or electronic shortcomings. Papers left about on desks can be picked up by cleaning crews. Computer files without effective access controls may be penetrated by unknown people who connect from across the country or across the world.

Does the company do the following?

* Know who is connecting when a network access is made
* Have established controls that implement access authorizations made by information owners

- Enforce good information marking and handling procedures for written and electronic forms
- Have a process to ensure that disclosure agreements are properly consummated whenever appropriate
- Manage and control authorized external accesses, such as for suppliers, consultants, customers, and others who may need sensitive information

SUMMARY

In a 1989 report in *ISSA Access*, Donn B. Parker of SRI International identified the major threats to information, in order of severity, as (1) loose talk, (2) observation or theft of printed or displayed information, and (3) attacks on electronic information.[11] Much information that is subject to unauthorized use is taken away in employees' memories and delivered to others in social chitchat. Another serious threat is the plain paper copier, which allows fast, easy duplication of sensitive documents. The computer threat is serious and growing. The worst vulnerability is employees' ignorance of the value of information to the company and their resulting failure to meet their responsibility for protecting it. Managers must recognize both threats and vulnerabilities to plan for appropriate information security measures.

NOTES

1.   Paraphrased from *The Lipman Report*, 15 March 1990.
2.   National Center for Computer Crime Data, 1989.
3.   *New York Times*, 2 September 1992.
4.   Paraphrased from United Press International, 27 April 1990.
5.   United States National Research Council, *Computers at Risk* (1991).
6.   *Information Security Monitor*, United Kingdom, July 1990.
7.   *Boston Globe*, 5 February 1990.
8.   *Austin American Statesman*, 23 June 1990.
9.   Donn B. Parker, *ISSA Access*, January–March 1990.
10. Morrie Gasser, *Building a Secure Computer System* (New York: Van Nostrand Reinhold, 1988), 89.
11. Donn B. Parker, *ISSA Access*, January–March 1990.

PART II

Protection of Information:
Concepts and Methods

4

Information Concepts

Information is an abstract concept. Managers know what information is, but many have difficulty understanding its value, development, delivery, and use. In this chapter information concepts are explained. The purpose is to build a conceptual foundation for managing effective information protection.

Information may be considered part of the process of the development of human know-how or knowledge. This learning process includes the development of knowledge in a sequence such as the following:

1. Data or experience—the raw material of knowledge, consisting of basic conceptual or representational elements that may not have been sorted or arranged in a useful or usable manner. Most people accumulate wisdom or savvy as they go through life. Much of this is in data form; we can put items together to come to conclusions about actions we see as beneficial.
2. Information—abstract representations of reality or concepts that have been organized to deliver useful knowledge. People (perhaps using computers) arrange data. Other people study or internalize the data and gain information. Conclusions from consideration of the information result in personal knowledge.
3. Know-how or wisdom—the result of repeated considerations of knowledge and of experiences in life that include using information. More books are now published every year than were produced in all of history before 1950. Collectively, these books supposedly represent the wisdom of humankind. Some of them probably result from fast publishing technologies and add little to knowledge, and many may be for purposes of entertainment.

Information also may be considered in terms of representation or form as opposed to the information itself, or knowledge. One's name is information; it can be represented in computer code, as a written signature, as a spoken phrase, as electrical signals.

FORMS OF INFORMATION

The commonly used forms of information are mental (memory or speech), electronic (in computer or communication systems), and written (including transparencies, photographs, and microforms).

CHARACTERISTICS OF INFORMATION

Information has a number of unique and interesting characteristics, many of which affect information vulnerabilities and information protection decisions.

- Information in electronic form may be moved at the speed of light. Although it is an intangible, in many cases such information has economic value the same as physical goods. Consider the banking system, which moves money around the world in the form of electronic signals. Simultaneous, instantaneous delivery of information is common. Consider television, with which everyone can watch the same sporting event in real time.
- Information is leaky. News spreads with bewildering speed. Organization theory is changing because everyone in a hierarchy can obtain the same information almost instantaneously. The boss no longer has privileged access to critical information. One of the principal security tasks is to try to maintain some privileges for organizational leaders. In one company, almost all the most interesting rumors came to United States employees from electronic contacts with employees in Europe.
- Information can be shared with others without diminishing its intrinsic value. We may not wish to share it, because sole possession may give us an advantage over others who do not have it. Today, information is the critical business asset; information makes the difference between profitability and failure. In many cases, however, information duplication means that more people gain benefit while the originator retains the benefit. Consider modern farming methods; when many farmers know how to use a method, the general welfare of the world's peoples increases.
- Information has synergy, that is, combinations of various sets of information, or innovative applications of information, can yield greater benefits. Many companies find that they can start new and profitable activities by using computer-based information already at hand for purposes of their core business.
- Information tends to have a brief useful life. The high technology world in which we live repeatedly generates new critical information sets. Some old information, like old news, may not be of much use. Information about the status of various business indicators is typical. Effective delivery of information is important. That is one reason why networks are widely used in business. The reliability of networks depends largely on proper security measures.
- Information can be efficiently and economically stored in bulk. Disk technology allows the storage of the entire contents of the United States Library of Congress on one platter. Database management systems provide fast, efficient retrieval of data in useful forms. Huge amounts of data can be carried around (and away) in a briefcase. A floppy disk can be put in a company envelope and mailed to an address outside the business, and the company pays the postage.
- Information lends itself to networking, allowing hundreds or thousands of people to share experiences, ideas, proposals, and concepts. In times past this was called folklore. Today, information sharing that previously took generations can be ac-

complished in a matter of hours. So-called shareware, computer software written by individuals and distributed free of charge over networks, now provides most programs used on personal computers. In large businesses with extensive employee-used networks, business, personal, and social information becomes intermingled and passed around. This data exchange often represents the real power structure of the company.

- Information ownership is difficult to establish and even more troublesome to maintain. Although small numbers of people may be expert in a given area, their knowledge once discussed, put on paper, or entered into electronic systems becomes generally known in a relatively short time. Computers, networks, telephones, and paper copiers all provide avenues for dissemination of information that someone may believe to be or hope to be private property (proprietary information). This need to claim ownership of information is one of the principal bases for concern about information security.
- Information increases exponentially. We are all in danger of drowning in a sea of information. If you receive mail—paper or electronic—you know that junk fills up all the available space. Sorting out what is useful is a Herculean task. The volume of information presented raises a risk that we may overlook or fail to protect something important while wasting time reading through trivia.
- Information is expensive. High technology companies estimate that their spending on information development, processing, and delivery amounts to about 5 to 7 percent of their annual revenues. For a company like IBM Corporation, this means an annual information cost of about $2 billion.

Information has interesting and challenging characteristics. These and other views of information allow us to plan information security.

THE BUSINESS ENTERPRISE AND INFORMATION UNIVERSE VIEWS

Understanding of the resource called information is essential if we are to develop proper security for it. Information is intangible, but at the same time it is a critical and expensive business resource. For purposes of information security, we can view the information resource in two ways.

First, information is a component of the overall business security responsibility (the *enterprise* view). That is, information protection is a subset of the management responsibility of the company director of security or equivalent position. Information is an asset that must be safeguarded along with employees, facilities, equipment, raw materials, product, and cash (see Table 4–1 a and b).

Second, information is a *universe*. We can picture how the information we wish to protect fits into the universe of all information. We wish to optimize investments; for security, this means identifying what is most valuable and then applying our limited resources there (see Figure 1–1).

Table 4–1a   The Enterprise View

Resources to Be Protected		
People	*Intangibles*	*Tangibles*
Employees	Information	Plant
Visitors	Reputation	Facilities
Travellers		Equipment
		Supplies
		Inventory

Table 4–1b   Forms of Information

Mental	*Written*	*Electronic*
Know-how	Paper	Computer core
Technical skills	Microforms	Transmissions
	Transparencies	Tapes, disks
	Photographs	Displays
Methods of Protection	*Methods of Protection*	*Methods of Protection*
Employee contracts	Marking and handling	Logical access
Nondisclosure agreements	procedures	controls
Contracts with suppliers	Storage procedures	Encryption
and customers	Destruction procedures	Marking and handling
	Physical security	of media
		Physical security
		Marking of displays

Business Enterprise: Information as a Security Responsibility

Responsibility for protection of business assets falls into three broad security categories—people, tangibles, and intangibles. Information protection, of course, is in the intangibles category. For information protection, as well as for other asset protection efforts, security work consists of the following activities:

- Management of security activities
- Physical security, or control of buildings and property, raw materials, work-in-process, products, and paper or media that contain information
- Human security, or safeguarding of employees and visitors during work and business travel
- Personnel security, or validation of employee hiring decisions through background checks, government clearance processes, and training
- Procedural security, or administrative security measures such as property passes, employee badges, registration and marking of documents

- Investigation into violations of policy or criminal behavior
- Electronic security, or the hardware and software that provide logical access control systems (identification, authentication, and authorization for computer accesses), closed-circuit television, and technical measures such as electronic sweeps for bugs

A company's overall security responsibility and the placement of the information security measures may be viewed by considering security within a business enterprise (Table 4–1 a and b).

Electronic information security is of the following two types:

- Computer security, or the protection of processes that involve the immediate operation and use of computers. This category includes data-processing centers and the use of intelligent workstations and microcomputers (see chapter 8)
- Communications security, or the logical and physical protection of network components such as computers, switches, and wires (see chapter 9)

Effective information protection occurs only when all three classes of information—mental, written, and electronic—and both categories of electronic information—computers and communications—are effectively safeguarded.

Information Security Attributes   Protected or safeguarded information has a number of attributes or characteristics. Donn B. Parker described these attributes as follows:[1]

- *Confidentiality.* Known only to a limited few; a set of rules or authorizations determines who may have, see, modify, or delete each information set.
- *Authenticity.* Genuine and conforming to fact; valid.
- *Integrity.* Unimpaired, complete, and whole; as correct and precise as the user expects it to be.
- *Utility.* Fit for the use intended; provides what the user needs to make good decisions.
- *Availability.* Presented and accessible when and where needed in the business operation.

In a general sense, *availability* involves protecting the information infrastructure, that is, the computers, networks, offices, laboratories, and other containers used to process, store, and deliver information. *Confidentiality* involves control of access to information. *Authenticity, integrity,* and *utility* usually depend on proper application and procedure design. However, there are many overlaps (see chapters 8 and 12).

The Information Universe

The information universe perspective (Figure 1–1) allows us to appreciate the need to direct our limited protection resources to the most appropriate targets.

Basic information protection is gained when sensitive or valuable company information is properly classified and protected according to established procedures for the assigned classification. There are two reasons for information classification:

1. Businesses simply cannot afford to protect every piece of information. Effective information protection, including establishing legal rights to information, is fairly expensive. Attempting to protect all company information is a waste of resources. Would a company want to spend money to make sure that the menu in the cafeteria is kept secret from outsiders? Classification identifies which information is to be protected and points to the established process to ensure adequate protection.
2. Unless established classification terms are used, that is, terms that are formally defined, are understood, and that have meaning to all employees, information is not protected. Casual terms such as *confidential, eyes only,* and *company information* may mean different things to different people. Protection occurs only when everyone who receives the information understands its value and sensitivity and then follows prescribed protection procedures.

Achieving a general understanding of classification purpose and meaning is a strenuous task. Information classification is the basic information protection measure. With related procedural requirements, classification is essential to information security. Classification is discussed in chapter 5.

Other Information Protection Measures

Copyrights and patents are supplementary information protection measures. Some copyrighted material and all patented material are publicly known. In addition to company classifications, there may be legal reasons to provide additional markings when information is shared under contract with outsiders. The following such marking is well known:

Copyright XXX Company, 1995; all rights reserved.

When information is used inside the company and also may be shared with clients, consultants, customers, or suppliers, it may be prudent to use both the company classification and a warning of a proprietary claim. Conversely, when a client or partner shares information, the receiving company should make sure that proper safeguards are established to protect the other party's data. In either case, the printed material, computer display, picture, microform, or other medium then shows two markings:

Company registered information.

and

Copyright 1995, XXX Company.
This material is unpublished work and is proprietary to XXX Company. All rights reserved.

The first marking is recognizable to company employees, if a proper job of training has been done, and tells them how to handle and protect the information. The second notice is for outsiders who may be provided with this material and who have signed a disclosure agreement but who do not know the rules. Legal requirements are explained in chapter 5.

SUMMARY

Managers need to have a good conceptual grasp of the resource called information. Otherwise, there is the risk that information may be treated as though it were "free" and unimportant to the company. An appreciation of information and its characteristics leads to the decision that information is a business resource that must be safeguarded.

NOTES

1. Donn B. Parker, *ISP News*, May/June 1995, 34.

5

Establishing Proprietary Rights to Information

Ideas mean money in today's world, since industry relies on technology to improve productivity. Your ability to do well or even survive in the resulting highly competitive climate will depend largely on your success in acquiring, protecting, and exploiting a piece of that technology. Your competitive edge also depends on how well you develop and protect your business information. . .

James H.A. Pooley, *Protecting Proprietary Business Information and Trade Secrets*, Probus Publishing, 1987

Information is an expensive and critical business resource. In fact, in today's highly competitive and rapidly changing business environment, information is the single most important business resource. As an intangible asset, information is difficult to control and protect. The methods and processes described in this book are examples of information security measures for prudent business managers attuned to the competitive world of today.

Information security consists of several levels of protective elements. These elements are the physical, logical, and procedural measures observed to some degree in most companies. However, another essential follows from the fact that information is an intangible, not a material, asset—that is, the company must take steps to establish its legal claims to information. A number of legal measures are aimed at staking a claim to ownership and can form the basis for a legal defense of ownership claims to information, should such be necessary.

Because laws vary from one jurisdiction to another, the discussion here is generic, but the measures recommended may be presumed to apply to the United States, Canada, and most countries of western Europe. In any case, business or security managers should not make decisions about information protection without expert advice from company legal counsel.

LEGAL MEASURES TO PROTECT INFORMATION

The title of this section is in some ways a misnomer, because only security measures actually protect information. Legal measures, on the other hand, are an attempt to establish a proprietary claim to certain information. Legal precautions and security measures work together to provide appropriate information protection. In most instances, legal or contractual measures applied to assuring ownership rights to intangible assets are used if information security fails or if parties to an agreement concerning the rights should be malfeasant. Once confidential information is exposed, it may be impossible to recover the benefits from its original condition of confidentiality. Although a lawsuit may recover damages, the value of the information and the advantages offered by exclusive knowledge of the information are lost.

Laws are only partially effective in preventing acts that society wishes to avoid. Peter Neumann of SRI International wrote the following:

> People are not deterred by a stiff penalty from indulging in profitable or enjoyable (but illegal) activity for which one has a low probability of being detected. Examples include sheep stealing in 18th century England which persisted although the penalty was hanging; and, a Jewish family's flight from Nazi Germany with the family jewels when removing assets (but not fleeing) was punishable by death.[1]

Establishing rights to information may involve a claim that information is a *trade secret*, is *copyrighted*, or is *patented*. A discussion of each of these claims follows. The word *claim* is used because proprietary rights exist only after a court of law has accepted the claim of the supposed information owner. In other words, one may claim that information XYZ is a trade secret. However, until such is proved in court, the supposed owner may not be aware that others have discovered information XYZ. Unknown parties may have a prior claim to the information, having developed XYZ independently.

This is a good time to note that it is always best to refer to your company's proprietary information (*proprietary information* and *intellectual property* are synonymous) by established company information classification titles. It is better to use the term *ABC Company Confidential* rather than *ABC Company proprietary information*. The former clearly identifies to employees the value of the information and the level of protection required for that information. The term *proprietary* indicates only that a claim is made to ownership. This distinction is important, as described in the following section.

TRADE SECRETS

The courts have generally defined a trade secret as information that has commercial value and is closely held. Assume that the ABC Company wishes to treat information XYZ as a trade secret and thereby establish a proprietary claim to it. The information must have some demonstrable *commercial value*. An announcement about the company picnic, plans to repaint the company automobiles, or the list of addresses of company facilities may be essential to business but may not necessarily have commercial value. A list of customers, especially those involved with product purchases, clearly does have commercial value. The decision whether information XYZ has commercial value may eventually rest with a court. In most cases good judgment by management—with legal counsel—should suffice to meet the first test.

Some courts have denied rights when no profit has resulted from exclusive possession of information. Merely holding a secret does not make it commercially valuable. Another challenge to ownership of a trade secret can occur if another company or individual has independently obtained the same information. Of course, a trade secret can be exposed and lose its value through employee carelessness.

Once the information is determined by a company to have commercial value, the company must then ensure that the information is *closely held*. This means that it is not widely known or generally distributed, *inside or outside* the company.

Requirements for Proving Rights to Trade Secrets

To establish proof that a claim to rights to a trade secret is justifiable, courts have generally held that the company claiming proprietary rights must be able to demonstrate that it performed three actions regarding the information. These actions are as follows:

1. The company identified which pieces of information among all those used in the business are valuable. It is not sufficient to claim that all information is valuable.
2. The company established a process for protecting the particular information identified as valuable.
3. The company must have sufficiently trained all employees so that the protection processes are generally followed across all operations of the company.

The last requirement is the Achilles' heel that frustrates many businesses trying to prove proprietary rights to information. Actions necessary to meet the second test for a claim of trade secret are closely aligned with security measures.

Identifying Which Information Is Valuable

One cannot protect everything. Just as householders cannot reasonably put all their belongings in a safe deposit box, businesses, because of cost and practicality, cannot protect all their information. The process of identifying which information needs to be protected is called *classification*.

Classification of information is a prerequisite to any legal claim that a piece of information is a trade secret.

Classification of information involves the following sequential processes:

1. The company must define its information classifications as appropriate to the business. Typically, companies identify two, three, or four classifications to suit business needs. Fewer classification titles mean less administration and lower costs. The classifications should be, at minimum, the following:

a. Highest, most sensitive level, restricted to named individuals
b. Midlevel, requiring moderate care, available to groups of people
c. Special category for information such as personnel records and medical records, restricted to the subject and authorized employees servicing the subject

2. The company must establish the protection procedure appropriate to each classification. These procedures must address creation of information (how to handle drafts, how to make and who makes the initial classification decision); information marking (many companies have designed classification logos implemented with rubber stamps, preprinted forms, and computer graphics); document and media security handling and storage rules; and destruction requirements at end-of-life.
3. All employees must be trained to follow the procedures. A situation in which some of the employees comply is useless in a legal context.

Classification Considerations and Procedures   A basic rule of management is:

Access to any company classified information is always based on need to know.

Access to information is never a right. It is a privilege based on job assignment and need to know. The assigned classification of a piece of information is a key element in making decisions about an individual's access privileges (higher classifications require more restrictive decisions). Table 5–1 illustrates a decision rule appropriate for granting access. There can be many variations depending on individual business circumstances.

Information managers or information owners (those responsible for granting access) must use such a decision rule, tailored to the business situation, to determine the access privilege appropriate to each employee. Decisions about access privileges should never be casual.

Once a specific level of access has been determined, the allowable privileges are determined as illustrated in Tables 5–1, 5–2, and 5–3.

Appropriate limitations of privilege for authorized computer system users are almost always required. These limitations may be implemented to further restrict indi-

Table 5–1   Decision Rules for Granting Access

Classification	Job Requirement	Need to Know	Named Individual	Authorization Level
Category 1 (highest)	Yes	Yes	Yes	Element or document
Category 2	Yes	Yes	No	Element or document
Category 3	Yes	Yes	No	File
Category 4 (lowest)	Yes	Yes	No	Any

vidual capabilities such as viewing, moving, modifying, or deleting information. These and more granular restrictions are triggered with security codes in the file or record header, or in the workstation identifier. The restrictions may include the following:

- Denial of print-out
- Denial of copying or forwarding
- Denial of modification
- Denial of erase
- Time limit on display

The Classification Process   The classification assigned to a file, element, document, or other form of information determines the level of protection to be provided. Classification is therefore an essential process in the prevention of unauthorized disclosure, modification, transfer, destruction, or loss of information access or services.

General responsibility for assigning a classification to information rests with the information owner—the executive or manager who has primary responsibility for the activity that generates or uses the information in question. A properly authorized manager or information owner must formally authorize the assignment of a classification. In practice, all employees who originate information have a responsibility to assign a classification promptly to ensure immediate protection.

Effective classification, which results in protection, has the following qualities:

1. Timeliness. Classification occurs with creation or initialization of the information (the act may be the expression of a physical reality into words).
2. Responsiveness to the actual or perceived value or sensitivity of the information. This judgment may be based on the knowledge or experience of the originator or information owner.
3. Consideration of the life cycle or anticipated uses of the information. Some information may be subject to greater risk. For example, information with a long life cycle must be assumed to have a greater probability of disclosure.

Illustrative Categories for Classification of Information   Classification categories establish the value or sensitivity of information elements, files, and documents. Each of the categories relates to specified protection levels.

Category 1 classification. Highest level, most secure. Usually called "registered," "restricted," or a similar term. Disclosure of information is limited to individuals identified by name by the originator or information owner.

Category 2 classification. Midlevel. Sensitive or valuable information restricted to individuals or groups who need the information because a specific job assignment justifies access.

Category 3 classification. Routine security. Information available only to individuals or entities authorized access by information owner consistent with need to know, job assignment, or contract.

Category 4 classification. Personal information (e.g., job applications, personnel records, medical records). Disclosure limited to subject, personnel officer, immediate supervisor, and legal counsel.

Unclassified. Information private to the company. May not be disclosed without authorization from the information custodian or public relations officer.

All information in all forms (mental, electronic, paper or other medium) must be subjected to classification. All information must be provided a level of protection appropriate to its assigned classification.

Risk-Threat Assessment   Threat scenarios and vulnerabilities analysis are essential to proper classification decisions. The appropriate information classification is best assigned by means of a *risk factor* developed in a risk assessment process. The risk factor is developed with a threat-vulnerability analysis matrix (Table 5–2). The risk factor is then applied in the classification decision matrix (see Table 5–3).

The Classification Decision Matrix   The determination of the appropriate classification category may be based on intuitive judgment and knowledge of the critical aspects of the business related to the information. In most cases, however, a better decision is made with the risk factor developed in Table 5–2 to identify an appropriate classification category with the matrix in Table 5–3.

Establishing Protection Procedures

The protection measures necessary to meet the requirement that information be closely held are security procedures that involve careful marking, handling, storage, and de-

Table 5–2   Risk Factor Derivation: Threat-Vulnerability Matrix

	Threat		
Vulnerability	*Known or Historically Realized*	*Suspected on Basis of Evidence or Observation*	*Not Immediate but Potential*
At some point in life cycle information changes form or is uniquely exposed	1	2	2
Information may be exposed because of variety of environment, situation of use, number of persons accessing	2	2	3
Information is routinely secure and modest vulnerability occurs	3	3	3

KEY: 1 = severe risk, 2 = moderate risk, 3 = routine risk.

Table 5–3   Classification Decision Matrix

		Risk Factor (from Table 5–2)	
	1	2	3
Effect of Loss*		*Classification*	
1	1	2	3
2	2	2	3
3	2	2	3

Category 4 (personal information) is always 1/1.

*KEY: The effect if information is disclosed, modified, or destroyed without authorization or if service or access is denied is as follows:

1 = Severe effect on operability, profitability, reputation

2 = Moderate, medium-term effect on profitability, programs, projects, competitive position

3 = Minor or short-term effect on business.

struction of company classified information in all forms. In several cases, companies that claimed proprietary rights to information had trouble establishing those rights when it was shown in court that processes for protection had not been established, thus failing the closely held requirement.

Case

Company A sued Company B when it discovered that Company B possessed technical data developed by Company A. During trial, employees of Company A admitted in testimony that managers at Company A seldom if ever said anything about information protection. The court held that the information was not closely held.

Ensuring That Procedures Are Generally Followed

Ensuring that procedures are generally followed is perhaps the most difficult test of all. The information owner is challenged to see that all employees—from top executives to mail-room workers—understand and follow the established information protection procedures required for each company information classification. Senior management must be committed to following the information protection procedures. Most leaks occur because senior managers are cavalier in handling information. Although executive secretaries may provide a first line of defense and might be relied on to make sure their bosses do what is right some of the time, executive arrogance combined with ignorance often results in careless or inappropriate handling of sensitive information. All employees must understand that careless handling of information and ignorance of the rules about information procedures are tantamount to financial carelessness or fraud.

Case

A traveling executive stopped to used a public telephone. In the telephone enclosure she found a copy of her company's secret operating plan. In most cases, fortune would have it otherwise.

COPYRIGHT

Copyright is a claim to exclusive ownership of the *arrangement* of a set of information elements. Copyright establishes absolute reservation of privileges. This book is copyrighted. Anyone can use the alphabets and words printed here, but the arrangement of the words is secured by copyright. Similarly, musical scores or computer software programs are copyrighted in the sense that the arrangement of the notes and the arrangement of the computer commands are subject to a claim of ownership.

Copyrighted information may be kept confidential and thus, if other tests are met, may be claimed as a trade secret. In such a case, the particular information set is protected by both a presumption of trade secret rights and a copyright. In other instances, copyrighted information (such as this book) may be made public. The decision about which legal protection measure or combination of measures is appropriate is one for discussion with legal counsel.

PATENTS

Patents are a claim to exclusive rights to and ownership of a process or device based on invention. The idea or process to be patented must be both new and useful. Patents may allow the established owner to sell licenses to others to share in the invention. All patents are made public as part of the issuing process. If the information is valuable mostly because it is secret, such as when a new process or machine allows a competitive advantage, the company may not wish to patent the invention but to hold it as a trade secret, using the company's information security processes to maintain secrecy.

Patents are expensive and time-consuming to obtain. Even when a patent is granted, difficulties may arise in defending a company's claims. It may be difficult to prove that the product that resulted from the patent actually did so. Other parties may submit claims to prior rights, that is, that they patented the same idea or process.

LIABILITY FROM MISHANDLING INFORMATION

The courts are viewed, at least in the United States, as a remedy for almost any wrong, real or perceived. It is not surprising that businesses that develop, process, hold, or deliver information must be concerned about lawsuits should expected information integrity or privacy be violated.

Most companies today, in their daily business, are part of what you might call an information chain. And that means that a major part of their business involves processing information and either using it to gain competitive edge, selling it, or passing it on in some way.

This point illustrates that information users depend on information providers for accurate and reliable data. Erroneous, confusing, or misleading information can result in bad management decisions, employee embarrassment, or client losses, and the business that provided the information can find itself in court. This information liability means that companies must make sure that proper controls are in place to maintain information accuracy, integrity, privacy, and reliability.

A number of cases, some published and others not generally known, illustrate the reasons for establishing effective legal claims to information, supported by efficiently implemented information security procedures. Some company names are fictitious, although the situations are true.

Case

On his last day of work at PDQ Company, an engineer asked his supervisor to help him carry several boxes to his car. Later, the engineer called from a distant city and offered to sell back to PDQ Company the plans for a new product. PDQ notified the United States Federal Bureau of Investigation (FBI), and the engineer was arrested and charged with interstate transportation of stolen property.

During the trial, however, the defense was able to show that PDQ Company's employees did not generally follow procedures for securing information. The engineer's supervisor at PDQ was shown to be an unwitting accessory to the theft, having assisted in carrying the information off the company's premises. The court decided that PDQ had forfeited its claim to the information as a trade secret, having failed to meet the tests to so prove.

Case

In *Motorola v. Fairchild Camera and Instrument Corp.*, the court noted that Motorola had failed to provide procedures for information protection and that as a result outsiders could see and operate supposedly secret machines and processes. The court subsequently invalidated Motorola's claim that certain information was protected and exclusive as a trade secret.

Case

A new company called VCS was formed by a number of scientists who formerly worked for Texas Instruments (TI). When TI discovered that the product proposed by VCS was exactly the same as a secret new product being researched at TI, a lawsuit quickly followed. In court, defense attorneys questioning TI employees found that the established TI information security procedures were not followed— in fact were ignored—in the high technology laboratories run by a brilliant technician described as "a scatterbrained mad scientist."[2] One TI employee in the labs said, "No one even mentioned security in general."

Because scientists were urged to publish, most of the sensitive material supposedly stolen by VCS had been published in scientific journals. Because of these security failures, it appeared that TI might lose the case. But the court eventually convicted two VCS employees of information theft on the basis of the fact that almost eight thousand files had been carried away from TI premises.

PROTECTING AGAINST COMPUTER CRIME

Although the more mundane security procedures that address control of pieces of paper and discouragement of loose talk remain the most important information protection methods, the risk of electronic pilfering is serious and will increase. In response to a number of highly publicized cases, various legal jurisdictions have adopted laws that aim to control unauthorized access to computer systems.

Computer crime laws have been established in forty-nine of the United States and in many other countries. In general, these laws have resulted from the democratization of computing; that is, a large and growing portion of the population of the world now has know-how and access to computers. This combination of skill and access presents opportunities to use computers against the interests of society.

Computer crime laws apply four factors in determining whether a particular computer action is a crime. These are as follows:

- *Knowledge.* The person who commits the act must be aware that he or she is doing something wrong. *Willful* and *intentional* mean about the same thing. The consequences of an action in which computers are used are a separate matter.
- *Purpose.* The person charged must be shown to have had a specific intent. Some laws say "who with the intent of committing fraud." In such a case unauthorized access not related to a plan to commit fraud would not be a crime. The intent must be an illegal one specified in law.
- *Malice.* The person must intend harm. It may be a defense for an accused if he or she can show that all that was intended was a harmless look. Some laws deal with this by saying that one who "purposely and without authorization accesses a computer and this action does not result in the alteration, damage, or destruction of data" commits a felony.
- *Authorization.* The person charged must not be authorized to access the computer. In some cases advertisements or telephone directory listings may be assumed to be authorization. A notice on first connection to the effect that "Unauthorized use is prohibited" may deal with this matter. Some laws require an "express consent by a computer owner as stated in an employee's job description, a contract, or other approval to use software, networks, computer systems, or property."

The last factor is one that can be dealt with by a company as a preventive measure. At sign-on or connect time, every computer screen display generated by company computers should clearly state that use of the computer is restricted, and that unauthorized use is unlawful. The computer screen should *not* issue a greeting nor should it provide any information about the company or type of computer or operating system being accessed.

A properly constructed initial screen display should read, for example, as follows:

WARNING: This computer is private property. Unauthorized use is forbidden. Violators will be prosecuted under the law.
PLEASE ENTER PASSWORD:

Computer crime laws are written to prevent the following:

- Electronic trespassing, in which an intruder simply browses in a system or network
- Theft of services, software, money, or goods
- Improper modification of data
- Damage to software or systems

Each jurisdiction has its own ideas about the importance of the various offenses and about appropriate punishment.

Recent laws address violation of privacy and one specific form of attack—computer virus software. Definitions used in the laws vary widely. One early problem that does not seem to have been satisfactorily resolved is the legal definition of *computer system*.

These matters reflect the relative ignorance of most lawmakers with regard to computing. Nevertheless, society has taken a strong stand that computers are essential to the functioning of human affairs. Laws no doubt have a deterrent effect, but a simple reading of crime statistics demonstrates that laws do not supplant the need for proper security measures. Laws do not necessarily speak to a most serious risk, the failure of trusted employees.

COMPUTER SOFTWARE PROTECTION

In 1991, computer software was estimated to be a $50 billion market. The computer industry is increasingly dependent on the software and service sectors for profit. This profitable and expanding market has generated a debate on the scope of intellectual property rights that may decide the winners and losers in the software market. The successful, innovative companies that are creating software want to preserve existing copyright principles. Conversely, the less successful software businesses seek to weaken copyright protection to allow copying of the "look and feel" of successful products without license payment or investment or risk of legal threats.

Copyright protection establishes the basis for intellectual effort (e.g., software) by promising reward. Copyright protection means the prevention of theft of intellectual property. The argument over the extent to which software should receive copyright protection usually takes place in litigation. But the debate is now taking place in legislatures and in international trade negotiations.

Successful companies in the software marketplace invest heavily in research and development (R&D) to produce innovative products. They rely on international intellectual property laws to protect those investments. Large computer businesses invest approximately 12 cents of every sales dollar on R&D.

Intense competition in the software marketplace forces successful companies continuously to develop next-generation technology. The bottom line is that wealth in the industry is no longer measured in terms of fixed physical assets, which are obsolete in three to five years, but in ownership of knowledge and technology. In other words, wealth is intellectual, not physical, property in the software industry.

The software situation reinforces the following reasons for establishing information protection measures:

- To prevent theft
- To discourage theft by establishing the value of trade secrets and by increasing the difficulty of theft and to establish the threat of prosecution
- To maximize the appearance of a company-wide program intended to meet the first two goals

SUMMARY

Advantageous aspects of law should be carefully considered and used to fortify a company's information security efforts. Prosecution of employees or outsiders for information theft, provided the company has established the basis for such, delivers a powerful message. Insiders and outsiders who know that vigorous punishment and prosecution are likely to follow information theft may be dissuaded.

Various forms of legal agreement (e.g., nondisclosure or disclosure agreements, employment contracts, covenants promising not to engage in similar enterprises) can strengthen a company's position if a lawsuit is necessary.

An effective and appropriate information protection program requires management commitment, careful selection of security measures, and good legal counsel to establish proprietary claims that reinforce security protections if legal action is necessary.

NOTES

1. Peter Neumann, Risks Forum, 1991.
2. *D magazine*, November 1986.

6

Information Protection Methods

Because information is a widely held intangible asset, protection methods span a range of activities, processes, administrative controls, and disciplines. Information security is a complex and everchanging specialty. Business managers should recognize that responsibility for information protection is not an extra duty to be assigned casually to anyone who has time.

INFORMATION SECURITY LEVELS

All information protection measures can be placed into one of the following three categories or levels:

Physical protection. Activities, procedures, equipment, and facilities that contribute to information security. Examples include safes, desk locks, door locks, document markings, storage facilities, security guards, and destruction procedures.

Logical protection. Computer-related or electronic security measures relating to information protection. These include logical access controls that implement identification, authentication, and authorization processes; access-control security software; encryption software and hardware; system monitoring and alarm software; and security processes built into computer operating systems, such as separation of users.

Procedural protection. Administrative activities that control and support limited access to information. These include marking of documents and computer displays with company information classification, distribution of encryption keys, management authorization to see and use information, management decisions concerning company classification of information, maintenance of authorization lists, establishment of a basis for legal claims to proprietary rights, security motivation and training of employees, development of ethical standards for employees, and publication of security directives (policies, standards, procedures).

INFORMATION SECURITY ELEMENTS

Within each level are security elements. Examples are given in the foregoing section. The selection of appropriate security elements and their effective application constitute the essence of information security work. Table 6–1 illustrates some common security elements.

Table 6–1   Security Elements

Security Level	*Typical Security Element*
Physical	Security access controls
	Guards
	Patrolling guards
	Access-control records
	Storage facilities (safes, cabinets)
	Observation systems (e.g., closed-circuit television)
Logical	Security software (operating system)
	Operating system user separation
	Personal identification or authentication software
	Computer access control
	Privilege control
	Activity logging
	Automated monitoring of system
Procedural	Granting authority to access
	Granting privileges
	Maintaining auditable records
	Classification process
	Information marking
	Information handling (e.g., mailing)

The basis for selecting security elements to be applied in a given situation is a function of the assigned information classification, the perceived risk, and cost. Chapter 12 illustrates the application of elements.

A high company information classification (indicating high value or high sensitivity) always requires strong protection. Usually, a high classification restricts access to the information to specifically identified individuals who have a need to know based on their business responsibilities. Highest classifications typically have names such as *Registered* or *Restricted*. Classification names are more useful when the name itself indicates the level of control required.

A high risk, even in the absence of company classified information, may justify strong protection. Consider a company that operates a large network of computers as the primary business management and control medium. Even if there is no company classified information on the network, the integrity and reliability of the network are vital to business operation and require strong security.

ANALYSIS OF RISK

A number of software packages and methods analyze risks to information and information systems and facilities. Some of these programs are fairly complex and apply mathematical techniques to offset the normal exaggerations that occur because of a dearth of reliable risk data. Almost all risk analysis procedures use a formula that approximates the following:

$$\text{Identified risks} \times \text{Value of risks} \times \text{Probability of event} = \text{Exposure}$$

In a very confined risk analysis, that is, an analysis that involves one facility, one computer application, or one local area network, such a process may yield useful information. Usually, this information regards potential breaches of security that may not have been noticed without the analysis. However, in terms of justification of security investments, the outcome of currently available risk analysis methods is highly questionable because of the paucity of historical information and the poor quality of the information that is available. In most businesses risk analysis is based on a series of expert guesses—unlike the insurance industry, in which vast data histories on automobile accidents, repair costs, liability payments, mortality, and fire experiences can be used to develop mathematically correct and financially reliable probabilities.

The lack of reliable historical data on information security occurs because most information security breaches or failures are kept confidential. Businesses do not air "dirty linen" unless the magnitude or scope of the security failure makes a cover-up impossible. Of course the result is that the public (and most information security experts) learn about only extreme losses. Disclosure of only large losses leads to erroneous estimates such as that each computer security crime costs an average of $500,000, a figure that is absurd.

In most instances, the expert estimates produced for security risk analysis are accurate only within one order of magnitude. One would hesitate to approach any financial officer of a company with data that are the result of the multiplication of a series of guesses.

DETERMINING SECURITY INVESTMENTS

Information security investments on the microlevel (local or application) may be assisted with a form of simple risk analysis. The most reliable basis for security investment is the information classification assigned by the company to the particular information sets at the site or in the particular application being considered. On a macrolevel, or company wide, investments are best determined by considering the highest information classes involved against the obvious risks. With or without formal risk analysis, the possibility that a serious risk will be overlooked remains. Knowledgeable information security personnel should be able to define the serious risks on the basis of general experiences reported by industry, government, and academia.

Case

A company was developing a payroll application. Certain data elements in the application were classified as *Company Personal* and others as *Company Confidential. Company Personal* was defined as requiring strong security. A cursory risk analysis showed considerable danger of embarrassment or violation of privacy should unauthorized people have access to *Company Personal* data. The application description showed a requirement for access by a number of people, including personnel managers and payroll clerks.

The information security elements selected were as follows:

- Encryption for *Company Personal* data when in storage on-line or when transmitted over networks
- Special user authentication and authorization processes that limited each authenticated person's access and actions to specific portions of the application files appropriate to that accessor's job and the employee population serviced by that person

Case

A large company in a high technology industry used an extensive network for engineering and business control. A series of attacks from computer hackers, which required frequent and costly rebuilding of systems and resulted in a loss of network reliability, made it clear that an immediate and unacceptable risk was at hand. The company made a quick decision to invest a large sum in the development of a security tool to test all computers in the network for compliance with the company's security policies.

Although company classified information was present on the network, this fact was irrelevant to the decision. There was a risk that the intruders could acquire data, but the justification for the investment was the risk to reliability and integrity of the network infrastructure.

The security investment decision included the following:

- Development of a new security policy applicable to all machines on the network
- Development of a security tool, in software, to test each node and make a report to appropriate management about the security status of each node, that is, the compliance with the policy. The tool also could be used locally to force compliance with essential security rules. In general, these rules involved software settings, defined through careful analysis of known attacks, which closed off opportunities for unauthorized parties to access network computers

NEED TO KNOW

Information protection becomes more difficult—and more costly—as the number of trusted people with access to company classified information increases. A rule is as follows:

> **Company classified information is provided only to employees who are both authorized to have it and, because of assigned job responsibilities, have a need to know.**

Curiosity or anxiety is never an acceptable reason to provide company classified information.

APPLICATION OF INFORMATION SECURITY ELEMENTS

The sample information security standards in Chapter 12 illustrate the application of information security elements in large businesses. In this chapter the individual security elements and their uses are discussed.

Physical Security Elements

Because almost all business information occurs in both written and electronic forms during routine business operations, physical security elements are always needed and always important. Physical security elements keep unauthorized people away from potential exposures to company classified information. A basic rule of information security is the following:

Always maintain an appropriate physical space between unauthorized people and company classified information in any form.

People who enter company facilities and who are not authorized employees should never be allowed in areas where they could see, pick up, copy, or otherwise access company classified information. Because most information theft occurs when pieces of paper are taken, this is a serious matter. The admonition applies to contract cleaners and to others who may have reason to be in an area but who do not have a need to know.

A logical rule from this observation is as follows:

Clean Desk Policy. All employees must lock away all classified information and turn off all displays when away from their workstations.

There is a dual responsibility for physical security. Management is responsible for keeping unauthorized people out of the workplace. Employees are responsible for protecting information in their care, in all forms. They should be trained to politely challenge, within the limits of their personal safety, any unrecognized person found in the work area—or to call security.

Physical security elements implemented as appropriate to the circumstances of the business operation include the following:

1. Physical control of human access to the area, building, office, or information-intensive spaces. This control may involve card or key access-control systems, guards, receptionists, closed-circuit television, proximity detection systems, or door locks.
2. Protection of information in computers, workstations or terminals, printers, facsimile machines, word processors, file cabinets, desks, or bookcases from unauthorized exposure, copying, or theft. Information on paper and removable media offer tempting targets. Unauthorized or disgruntled employees are as much a threat as paid industrial espionage agents. Casual passers-by have been known to sign

on to an employee's idle workstation and enter a program that delivers the employee's account identity and password to a remote device.

3. Protection of the information infrastructure, including locking telecommunications equipment rooms or closets, special physical access controls, and security protection for laboratories, data centers, communications centers (including switchboard operations), and similar facilities. Protection of all electronic and computer-based information devices that may be included in manufacturing, engineering, design, and general office areas.

Logical Protection of Information

At the logical level, security elements include all computer hardware and software security functions and processes. Some logical security elements are software systems embedded in or added to computer operating systems, which provide identification, authentication, and authorization of people or programs.

Management controls are intended to guide operations in proper directions, prevent or detect mischief and harmful mistakes, and give early warning of vulnerabilities. Organizations in almost every line of endeavor have established controls based on the following key principles:

Individual accountability
Auditing
Separation of duty[1]

Computers can be programmed to implement these essential controls. Individual accountability fixes responsibility for a particular action. In a complex business operation, many circumstances might lead to actions that are, in the end, contrary to management intent or purpose. Other actions may be taken in bad faith or for mischievous purpose. To maintain control, managers must be able to fix responsibility even though there was no direct supervision when the incident occurred.

These identification, authentication, and authorization systems are called *logical access-control systems* and provide the following three functions:

*   *Identification* is a claim of identity made by a person or a program early in the process of connecting with a computer, system, or network. This may be a name, an employee or program number, or an alias. It can also be a more secure identifier such as a secret code or expression.
*   *Authentication* is the process by which a computer determines whether the claim of identity is genuine. In most cases, the person or program claiming an identity presents a token to the computer. A *token* is something the person or program has, is, or knows. It can be a password, a plastic card (perhaps with a microcomputer embedded in it), a fingerprint or voiceprint, a retinal scan, or an encrypted code (more typical of a software program). By examining an established reference file in the

computer, the security system compares the offered token to the claimed identity. If a match is obtained, the person or program is authenticated.

- *Authorization* is the process that enforces established access rights once the requesting person or program is authenticated. In other words, the security system limits what the person or program may do. These limits (or rights or privileges) are set by the information owner or custodian. The options are authorizations to do one, any combination, or all of the following: read, move, modify, or delete. The rights or privileges may apply only to specified files or information elements, or they may be general to all files in a system.

Authorization is a means to establishing *separation of duties*, the process that requires that two or more trusted people review and approve an action. As an illustration, consider a payroll file. The payroll staff may be authorized to read all files, but only a specific payroll technician is authorized to modify a file and probably only files for certain people. If only one or two people were authorized to print payroll files, the authority to print checks from the computer would be tightly controlled.

This type of control or authorization is called *discretionary access control.* *Mandatory access control* is usually found only in military systems in which specific, individual security clearances lead to privileges that are compartmented. Such a system is beyond the intent of this book.

For particularly important or business-sensitive matters, management may wish to establish a strong form of authentication. This is usually referred to as *nonrepudiation.* This is the logical equivalent of legal notarization of a signature on a document. Digital signatures, which use cryptographic methods, are an illustration of nonrepudiation.

Auditing and record-keeping security software may include the following functions:

- Checking to make sure that a particular system is in compliance with established company rules
- Keeping records of all accesses or unsuccessful accesses
- Sounding alarms or contacting security staff if suspicious activities occur

Some security audit systems use so-called artificial intelligence to compare ongoing events with collected records of normal activities. When an unusual event occurs, the software makes reasonably informed decisions about several alternative reactions, such as to continue watching, to go into a higher state of control, to shut off a process, or to notify security of an emergency. Advanced security audit systems can defend themselves if a penetrator recognizes the presence of such a system and attacks it.

Other logical security controls include hardware or software features that separate users and files, isolate security functions, and enforce least privilege. *Least privilege* means that any person or program is given only the absolute minimum rights or privileges to perform the authorized function. Least privilege applies to hardware functions, operating system functions, application programs, and human access to systems or data.

In his book *Building a Secure Computer System*, Morrie Gasser identifies the characteristics of good logical security systems. The systems should be friendly, that is, "Security should not affect users who follow the rules. It should be easy for users to give access . . . [and it] should be easy for users to restrict access."[2] Gasser also points out a most important consideration. We should never depend on "the secrecy of any part of the system's security mechanisms."[3] The only safe assumption is that an attacker knows everything about the security of the system. Making system functions known to a wide audience allows many people to test the system, and to comment on possible weakness, which can be fixed. A secret process may have weaknesses known only to an enemy. We must not forget that all software has errors.

Another form of logical security is the *kernel*. This is software (and possibly hardware) that is separate from the general operating system. A kernel runs much like an operating system but is written to be as simple and brief as possible, so that its functions can be verified or proved reliable. Again, all software has errors, and large programs are almost impossible to prove error-free. A kernel can perform some of the critical authentication, authorization, and auditing functions described earlier.

Encryption software and hardware are logical security elements. *Encryption* is use of a cipher, or translation, to a code based on a cipher key and a complex algorithm. Once data are changed to an encrypted form, decoding (or decryption) is extremely difficult unless one has the same or complementary key.

Encryption (the field is called *cryptography*) provides strong protection against eavesdropping on network circuits or picking up electromagnetic radiation from computer equipment. These espionage techniques are neither difficult nor expensive. Eavesdropping requires only the connection of wires to a circuit carrying data. Radiated signals—given off by all computer devices—can be picked up through walls or windows. Use of these techniques with slightly modified home television equipment has been demonstrated. A particular threat is with the use of cellular telephones, which involve the broadcasting of conversations over a wide area. Teleconferencing has the same problem—the "footprint" of the downward signal of a satellite is large enough to be picked up by many unauthorized people, perhaps using home equipment.

Case

An executive was participating in a company videoconference between upstate New York and California when he received a call from his aunt in Kansas. She had picked up the conference on her dish antenna and had called her husband in from the fields to see their nephew in action.

Case

A large New York bank hired a security firm to attempt espionage against the bank's cash transfer system. The agents dressed as telephone repair workers and entered the basement of the bank's headquarters in New York City, where they proceeded to attach eavesdropping equipment. They were challenged by a guard but were not further bothered after assuring the guard that they were "testing data center circuits." They succeeded in copying traffic on the lines, breaking the code used, and shocked the bank's chairman by presenting him with convincing evidence of the vulnerabilities of the system in use.

The following rule applies to encryption:

Information assigned the highest company classification must be encrypted when on networks and when in medium- or long-term storage on network-accessible devices. Encryption should be considered for telephone circuits regularly used for sensitive executive decision-making.

Electronic sweeps or tests for planted listening devices in telephones, windows, and walls are an essential part of information security. Company offices cannot be assumed to be safe. It is not uncommon to find taps on telephones or implanted listening devices in hotel conference rooms. These may be simply leftovers, but the threat is real. A rule is as follows:

All facilities or spaces where critical management decisions are made should be periodically checked for hidden devices.

Procedural or Administrative Information Security Elements

Procedural security elements lack glamour and constitute rather tedious work. They are regularly ignored. This failure to pay attention to the more mundane security tasks constitutes the single greatest cause of information security failure.

Among the important procedural or administrative information security elements are maintaining current information access authentication and authorization records and cutting off privileges as the job situation dictates. The company's personnel practices should include effective out-processing for employees who leave. Information security considerations should be addressed automatically and routinely during this process.

When employees leave the company, are their computer accounts promptly canceled? Are former employees allowed back into the work environment? Do employees about to leave the company continue to have privileges to see and use information right up to the last moment?

A useful example of an efficient process is one used by Xerox of Canada. Every day, data from the employee master record was matched against the security profiles that showed information authorizations. The match included employee number, job code, and location code. Any change or failure to match immediately suspended the employee's (or former employee's) privileges.

Case

A highly-regarded computer programmer resigned from her job. Some months later the company controller noticed that disk storage costs had increased considerably. A review of disk storage charges showed that large amounts of space were being used by the account assigned to the former programmer, who had opened a consulting business at home and had been routinely storing her customers' files on the company's system.

SUMMARY

Attention to detail is critical in any important endeavor. For information security, "the devil is in the detail" is an apt saying. Effective security depends on careful selection and application of security elements from the three levels and requires continued periodic monitoring and auditing to ascertain that all protections remain in place and in effective working condition.

NOTES

1. *Computers at Risk: Safe Computing in the Information Age*, (National Research Council, 1991).
2. Morrie Gasser, *Building a Secure Computer System* (New York: Van Nostrand Reinhold, 1988), 52.
3. Ibid., 53.

7

Securing the Information Environments

Some business environments create more risk to information than do others. In this chapter some of the environments in typical business operations are discussed, and the information security considerations for each are explained. This discussion should be useful in determining information protection standards for a given situation, department, or company. More detailed information security requirements applicable to these environments are presented elsewhere in this book, especially in chapters 8 and 12.

THE OFFICE

The office is an information factory involved in creating information and in changing the form of information. Both these activities imply critical information security responsibilities.

Creating information means that new or changed information is developed and published in some form. Along with creation goes the decision about assigning the proper company information security classification. Without proper classification there is no protection.

Case

An executive went on an extended trip to an area of the world where his company had not previously operated. On return, he wrote a report detailing competitors' operations in that area and explaining the strategic opportunities, strengths, and weaknesses of his company. He sent the report to a distribution list of people he thought would be interested. He did not, however, classify the information, and the report was widely copied, forwarded, and electronically distributed to hundreds of people. The executive or his secretary should have known better. The people in hundreds of offices who read it and sent it on should have recognized the sensitivity of the report. In all probability, the report was provided to outsiders.

Change of form means that information is transformed from mental form into written or electronic form, from electronic to written form, or from written form to electronic form (scanning). Because information is at risk when it changes form, the office poses a severe information security challenge.

Case

Order processors were taking telephone calls from customers and entering product orders into a shipping and billing system. A clerk discovered that she could correct errors after a shipping order was made. She set up false orders, which released products to her boyfriend, and then reversed the orders. The change from mental or oral form (the called-in order) to electronic form provided an opportunity for fraud.

Office Information Security Measures

For purposes of this discussion, an *office* is defined as any place where knowledge workers process and handle information, usually on an individual basis. Laboratories, engineering units, accounting activities, administrative services, and similar business functions fall within this category. Managers, professionals, secretaries, and clerical workers must be trained in the company's information protection procedures. These must include instructions for the following:

1. Recognizing valuable or sensitive information and promptly assigning the most appropriate company information classification. This applies both when information is created and when it is received from others who may have failed to establish proper protection. Local security staff should be informed to take action with the originator or sender in the latter case.
2. Marking, handling, storing, and destroying documents or electronic files as appropriate to their value or sensitivity, as indicated by information classification. These procedures should be specified in the company information security standards.

Electronic forms of information, such as documents displayed on computer screens or sent over networks, usually require special marking and handling instructions (see chapter 12). Electronic information security procedures may be limited (classification page markings cannot be affixed) or enhanced (graphic classification labels can be applied) by the particular systems applications and services at hand.

Using Computers in the Office

In an ideal world, a microcomputer used in an office, laboratory, or engineering facility should offer excellent security. For example, with today's software capabilities, an efficient office system should do the following:

1. Force the document writer to make information security decisions by requiring that the writer choose a company information classification before filing or sending a document; or by declaring the material unclassified.
2. Encrypt the document or message automatically should the highest information classification be chosen and provide for decryption by the addressee.

3. Enforce the rules concerning the classification selected, perhaps by preventing forwarding by addressees, blocking out options to use certain addresses (e.g., out of the company), or limiting distribution to established groups who have a need to know in certain subject categories.

Unfortunately, most systems do not provide these ideal security features. Users are forced to develop and use manual procedures to ensure information protection.

Logical Access Control

A key security measure is identification and authentication of each user. In many offices and laboratories, however, microcomputers are used without any security protection. Anyone who happens along can sign on and access whatever files may be at hand. Individual users usually choose not to implement security measures until after a disaster has occurred.

Carefully observing the rules for using passwords makes it fairly certain that unauthorized parties are not able to sign on to or otherwise access office computers, files, or mainframe computers connected to the office by means of networks.

Prudent passwords have the following qualities:

- Contain at least eight characters
- Mix alphabetic, numeric, and special characters
- Cannot be found in a dictionary (modern hackers use the dictionary word list to search quickly for matches with passwords)
- Are kept secret by the user
- Are changed periodically to new and different words or phrases

Chapter 8 presents details on authentication precautions, use of passwords, and other prudent measures.

The Virus Threat

A "virus" program can be as brief as eight or ten lines of code, which appends itself to other programs and which may cause mischief or destruction. "Infections" resulting in damage to computer files have become commonplace. The computer virus problem will reach epidemic proportions and cost from $5 billion to $10 billion in system downtime and recovery expenses during the next five years.[1]

The data that support this statement were developed with the Tippett Curve, a mathematical equation. Instructions on how to make a virus program are available from computer bulletin boards, descriptive articles, so-called software toolkits, and even from a mail-order source. Motivation for making and distributing harmful viruses ranges from demonstrations of technical prowess to revenge against employers or co-workers and fraud.

A company must establish rules about the use of so-called freeware or unapproved software in company computers. At some businesses, employees sign a special employment contract that covers the use of company computers. The contract specifies restrictions on which programs may be used. Every business should have an established process for vetting all new software before it is put into use. Virus screening packages are available for this purpose.

Using Copiers

The plain paper copier, first delivered by Xerox in the mid-1950s, revolutionized the office by eliminating carbon paper and allowing broadcast communications using paper. Instead of the old circulation slip, each recipient received a copy, and all recipients received copies at about the same time. This function is now largely assumed by electronic network mail services.

The copying machine was also the greatest boon in history for industrial spies, who could now make a copy of a valuable document and spirit it away. Because the original was still where it belonged, company managers had no way of knowing that the information had been stolen. With a properly configured computer, however, there may be evidence that an access was made and that information was improperly moved or modified.

Special red paper is available that cannot be read by a copier. However, it is not convenient to use in some applications, and the readability often is poor.

Company information protection rules should set requirements for which classifications of information may and may not be copied. In some restricted-access areas—where highest priority information is common—the use of copiers may be restricted by requiring the use of a token or other user identification mechanism. In some cases, serial numbers are engraved on the copiers' platen glass, providing a record of the machine on which each copy was made.

Like networks, copiers represent an information vulnerability; employees may make copies of information for people who are not authorized to see it. Sometimes the combination of an improperly sent electronic message and a copier is a path to information exposure. Extra or spoiled copies, carelessly discarded, may provide the means for a leak. Forgotten originals frequently are found and used by unauthorized parties.

Case

A company executive wrote a memo about a potential personnel action that had been discussed by the board of directors. The executive sent the memo to several other senior managers for review and failed to mark it with the appropriate company classification for such a sensitive piece of information. The memo was forwarded to many other people—who had no need to know—through the company's electronic mail network. One of these people made printouts. One of these printouts was copied and provided to a national newspaper, which printed it. The company president had to explain the situation in memos to the employees and to the newspaper. The effects of the entire incident were embarrassing and upsetting to the employees and the company.

Using Facsimile Machines

Industrial espionage agents find the ubiquitous facsimile (fax) machine to rival the plain paper copier for ease of use in stealing information. S.L. Berry called the phenomenon "faxpionage" and claimed that bugging of fax transmissions and easy access to fax printers by casual passers-by represent a severe information security threat.[2]

Another threat to the "smart" or microcomputer-controlled fax is hackers breaking in and diverting messages to unauthorized addressees.

Facsimile machines should be used only in controlled areas. If sensitive information is to be faxed, the sender should make certain that the identified addressee is standing by at the receiving machine. Facsimile devices that routinely carry sensitive information should encrypt the information while it is in transmission.

Videoconferencing

The full-feature, real-time videoconference allows efficient meetings to be held among people who are in various distant locations. It allows convenient exchange of information, display of graphics, and exchange of documents. Security for videoconferencing is especially critical because the technology used—typically involving satellite transmissions—presents a very large footprint on the downlink side. This means that the conference signal can be picked up by parties remote to the receiving station.

All videoconference network traffic should be encrypted. The encryption should be provided as part of the video and voice circuit services of the supplier. The encryption key for the videoconference facilities should be protected at the highest company classification level. The company information classification that applies to any information used in a videoconference should be clearly indicated to all the participants, and all graphics or documents used should be properly marked.

Videoconference facilities should be physically secured. Participants should be able to anticipate complete privacy during their meetings. If external (outside the company) videoconference facilities are used, the contract for such use should stipulate the security provided and guaranteed.

Physical Security for the Office

I am going to teach you, whether wearing a three piece suit or wearing a lovely gown, how to go through somebody's garbage.
William Dear, private detective trainer

Prudent practices regarding clean desks and sign-off of workstations or computers when the user is away from the workplace are important. Most security breaches occur because of employee ignorance or carelessness. Leaving sensitive documents on a desk or displayed on a workstation is an invitation to exposure.

Case

Three men stole various documents dealing with the manufacture of "Lycra" fiber from DuPont. Later they offered to return the materials for a $10 million payment. As a result of a sting operation conducted by Swiss police and the FBI in Geneva in February 1989, the men were arrested.[3]

Of course the company should control access to all work areas, including offices. Communications or telephone closets and switch rooms and private branch exchange facilities offer tempting opportunities for information eavesdropping and should be secured the same as computer equipment.

Trash and unwanted documents (which may be extra copies of valuable documents or contain obsolete but still useful information) must be properly handled. All paper and media trash should be destroyed on-site before anyone not in the company's employ can obtain it. Or it should be handed over in a controlled manner to a bonded destroyer, who certifies to its reduction to pulp or ashes.

Case

During processing of accounting summary reports in a data center, several reruns were necessary because of processing errors. Later, the wastepaper was hauled to a certified destruction service. However, an employee failed to close the doors on the truck, and hundreds of sheets containing sensitive information were found blowing about on the city streets by the company treasurer as she drove to work the next day.

Conference Rooms

Just as employees in all company offices should observe clean-desk practices, so should all conference rooms be cleared of any documents after a meeting. Blackboards and flip charts should be left clean. The sponsor of any meeting should understand it to be his or her responsibility to leave the room cleared of business material.

If information assigned a top level classification is discussed, the meeting sponsor should be required to keep a list of those present. Being told information is a disclosure is the same as receiving a document.

SECURITY IN BUSINESS COMPUTER APPLICATIONS

All too often security is considered only after an application is developed and implemented, perhaps at the auditors' first operational review. It is better, less expensive, and easier to provide security when an application is first designed or programmed (see chapters 8 and 12).

At a minimum, security should be an inherent part of the process of application development, built into the phased development process. Information security decisions during application design and development can take place only after someone has made a decision about the value, or company information classification, to be assigned to the data used by the programs in the application. Information system development, programming, and operations managers are only caretakers of company data. The data owner is typically the senior manager responsible for (or budgeting for) the application. This manager must be required to make information classification decisions before the appropriate security decisions are made at key points in the development cycle.

A rule is as follows:

Only the data owner can make decisions concerning information value and sensitivity (i.e., decide which company information classification applies to a file). Only the data owner has authority to make access authorization decisions.

Systems development and maintenance are ongoing management processes that extend over the life of an application. Security is inherent in several phases of development of an application.

Information Security in the Application Development Phases

In a typical business application development phased-management process, there are seven phases, with security checkpoints in each, as follows.

Phase 1—Project Initiation

The designer, working with the application user and data owner (not necessarily the same people) must determine if any information in the application should be classified and, if so, what level of protection is required. Control and marking of outputs, displays, and reports should be addressed.

Phase 2—Design

During functional design, the application designer must ensure that proper security needs have been identified and that any special or nonstandard security features are identified. In some cases, a security package offered by the servicing data center may not suffice. Protection for all system processes must be provided, including data acquisition, data conversion, processing, storage, outputs, displays, editing, reporting, printing, and delivery. Manual processes, from a security viewpoint, are as important as automated processes.

Phase 3—Specifications

System specifications must address the correctness of security processes relative to information classification by the data owner. Access-control processes and checks, edit or audit responsibilities, and reactions to deficiencies noted during operations must be clearly identified.

Phase 4—Procedures Development

Quality programming supports security. This means that program code should be written in short, structured segments that allow effective review. Software errors can become security disasters. Detailed procedures must be written to ensure continued control and integrity throughout operation of the application. Contingency plans for reliable operation and recovery in the face of problems such as power failure or surges, fires, floods, and inappropriate employee actions must be developed and tested.

Phase 5—Installation

The servicing data center or distributed environment must conduct reliability and acceptability tests of the application before accepting it as production. This includes validation of run instructions, checking output for correctness, testing recovery processes, and obtaining user quality sign-off. A procedure must be provided for management control over all application changes, emergency and routine.

Phase 6—Maintenance

Program maintenance, always a difficult issue, must be well managed. Management must include checking for effects on information security every time a change is proposed.

Case

A programmer made an emergency change to a sort routine during nonworking hours. The following morning, the application was run and reports were mailed to customers. Later, it was discovered that a programming error had resulted in intermingling of customers' data. Some customers were upset that competitors may have obtained information about purchases.

Phase 7—Revisions and Replacements

If the application is revised or replaced, the security checkpoints must be fully reapplied. Because the situation in which the application is used probably has changed, the original information protection measures may no longer be acceptable, and the company's information security standards may have changed.

The Data Center–Communications Center

In years past the data center was the principal information depository, and as such received intense security attention. With today's distributed systems and the general availability of network-connected computing on desktops and at home, information security is diffused over almost the entire company. Nevertheless, the data centers and the associated communication centers require special attention (see chapters 8 and 9 for more detail).

Mainframe computing, contrary to some reports, is far from dead. Even the most distributed of systems requires databases for storage, batch processing, and orderly retrieval of information. These large databases with the associated volume-processing runs, such as a personnel database and payroll system, require large computers and specialized facilities. Likewise, large networks may require centralized control and monitoring capabilities, also usually provided in a specialized facility.

These buildings, rooms, or areas require sufficient security to assure protection of the hardware, control of access to computer or network consoles, and protection of the data media in use or stored there. Contingency planning and testing are additional key elements of management of data-processing and communication facilities. Logical access-control systems are required to prevent unauthorized changes to programs or unauthorized access to data. A quality control process is needed to ensure that application and operating system software loaded into the mainframe computers is suitably tested for integrity, reliability, usability, and freedom from unauthorized changes.

Physical Security in the Data Center–Communications Center

A good general rule is that only authorized computer or communications workers and maintenance workers—those required to perform necessary tasks—be allowed into computer facilities. There always seems to be a reason to allow other people into these places, but the reason for such an exception is seldom valid.

Digital Equipment Corporation runs many of its data centers in lights-out mode; there are no people in the center. Clever software monitors operations, provides remote maintenance analysis, and can even call the appropriate manager at home should things begin to go wrong.

Visitors should always be logged in and escorted when they are within controlled areas. If computer or software maintenance technicians are from outside sources, that is, from the company's computer suppliers, their presence, time-in and time-out, and exactly what they do should be carefully recorded and reviewed by appropriate managers. This is as much for good management control as for security. Prudent care for information dictates that such technicians not be allowed to operate or come and go at will.

Logical Security Measures for the Data Center–Communications Center

The computer itself should record who is operating the system and should make a log of all the security-relevant actions taken. These include starting and completing jobs, file accesses accepted and refused, control points, and all operator-initiated references or changes to the operating system software.

Any modification to job control language, job parameters, application programs, and operating system software should go through prior management review and detailed operations quality control. This process must ensure that the actions taken are properly authorized and that the changes work as described in documentation and do not threaten systems or data integrity. Emergency requirements for software fixes should be handled in a way that allows a quick response but that avoids permanent changes to the operating environment until the control process can be completed.

Although security experts at one time believed that skilled technicians posed a threat, experience seems to indicate that most computer technicians are trustworthy. Good management control remains a necessity, however, and may be one reason for the good performance of so many technicians. All accesses to data files should be authenticated by the operating system. For the purpose of security, an application program is treated the same as a person. In fact, an application program may well be a covert agent of a person, and the program's purpose might be unauthorized. So both programs and people must be identified, authenticated, and authorized to read, move, or modify data.

The Network

For our purposes, the *network* is considered to include all directly connected computers and devices. Therefore, network security depends on the security of all nodes connected. One weak link, even in a network of tens of thousands of nodes, can mean that a company could lose the use of a critical business facility (see chapter 9).

Security for a network may be viewed from several perspectives, such as type of access; delivery mode for logical access control; and design of the network structure. Designs include point-to-point, star or tree, hierarchical star, mesh, and ring. A local area network or a wide area network may be constructed with any or several of these designs.

Warning Screens on Network Connection   To establish proprietary rights to information, and to allow prosecution should such be warranted, all electronic accesses to network facilities should immediately result in the display of a warning screen. This screen or display should not give a welcome notice, nor should it provide information helpful to a would-be penetrator.

A proper warning-screen notice reads as follows:

WARNING: THIS IS A PRIVATE NETWORK. ANY AND ALL UNAUTHORIZED ACCESS IS PROHIBITED. VIOLATORS WILL BE PROSECUTED UNDER THE LAW.

Enter identification:
Enter password:

An improper screen might read as follows:

WELCOME TO ABCompany network.
If you need help call 123-4567

Enter identification:
Enter password:

The latter screen is unacceptable because it could establish a legal right to use, even for someone not authorized, by offering an invitation. It also provides too much information—the name of the company and a help number—both of which might be extremely useful to a skilled hacker.

Case

A company advertised a service in the telephone book. The password for access to the service computer was the same as the name of the company. Hackers gained control of the computer by using HELP commands.

Logical Controls in Networks Regardless of network topology, the security system wants to know who is connecting and what the caller is permitted to do. At one level, all networks are public and all share common facilities. That is, because of common use of public utility circuits (AT&T, GTE, British Telecom, French PTO), it is almost impossible to prevent someone unknown from entering the worldwide interconnected maze of circuits. However, before a person unknown can reach a process or information, there should be a challenge that results in identification, authentication, authorization or, if those tests are failed, rejection, and creation of an audit record.

When networks are used, identification and authentication become critical security processes. Unlike situations in which all computers and access points are contained within one building, allowing physical checks and controls of entry, a network allows invisible entities (people or programs) to attempt access.

Passwords have many weaknesses and may be easily compromised or spoofed. Additional means for reliable authentication include voice and fingerprint analysis, retinal scans, and the use of smartcards.

A smartcard, or microprocessor embedded in a plastic card, provides a possible resolution of the identification and authentication issue. The July 31, 1989, European edition of *Newsweek* described a "supersmartcard" that has a keyboard and display and can store data containing artwork, photographs, and thousands of pages of information.[4]

The logical access-control or security process used by the connected nodes of a network might be in one place where all identification and authentication requests are handled. Or, as in the Xerox Network System (XNS), access controls might be fully distributed to every node connected. Or, security controls might be at several critical network switching centers. Each method has problems and advantages that are beyond the scope of this discussion.

When each node contains its own security-control process, the worry is whether all the nodes on the network have established suitable security parameters. At Digital Equipment Corporation, a software tool called INSPECT (Interactive Network Security Policy Examination/Compliance Toolset) was developed to reside with the operating system on every node and to measure compliance with the company's established computer security standards. The tool automatically sends reports of noncompliance to various management entities, ensuring that weaknesses are made evident. An optional mode allows the node system manager to use the tool to "lock down" or force compliance.

When a network uses security control at the central database, security software such as IBM's RACF (Resources Access Control Facility) allows for logical security measures and provides individual user profiles. Computer Associates software packages called ACF2 and Top Secret provide similar functions.

Various security measures such as "smart" modems can be built into network devices. These are actually microcomputers that are placed in the line between the user attempting a connection and the service computer. The call-back modem, for example, receives a request for service and identifies and authenticates the caller. The system then hangs up and calls the authenticated user at a predefined telephone number. An authorization process then allows certain privileges to the caller, who is assumed at that point to be genuine.

An integral part of network management is monitoring of security status. Although network management centers always monitor line quality and availability, security may be a secondary issue. Several suppliers of network management systems now offer security monitoring capabilities among other services provided.

Transmission Security   So far we have discussed obtaining access to computers by use of networks. But what about the danger that someone unknown, by tapping communications circuits or by picking up emanations or satellite downlink transmissions, may eavesdrop on messages as they pass a point in the network? The only reliable security for data in transmission is ciphering or encryption. Unfortunately, computer manufacturers have not yet provided an economical and easy-to-use encryption service. There is no technical reason why. One explanation is that the market is not ready to buy encryption. Cryptographic products, for example the initial set of IBM encryption products, have not sold well.

THE LABORATORY

Most companies consider the laboratory a critical installation with high-value information. Special access controls—physical and logical—may be appropriate when a laboratory includes information or devices the business considers to be proprietary or that are viewed as being competitively sensitive.

Scientists and engineers tend to be free thinkers. They are not impressed by—and often resist—any kind of control. As a result, many companies have lost critical competitive advantages when scientists or engineers have presented papers to professional societies and revealed ground-breaking research or developments. Scientists and engineers also may believe they are immune from the risks that beset others.

Case

Dr. Z was a scientist at a large computer manufacturer. He frequently worked at home. His children also used the home computer. One night while working late on an important project, Dr. Z spilled coffee on his floppy disk. "Lucky for me," he thought, "I made a back-up!" But when he went to use his back-up, Dr. Z found to his dismay that one of his children had written over his precious data with a computer game. The work was lost.

In another case, scientists gave a guided tour to fellow experts from a competitive company with the understanding that the courtesy would be returned. To their chagrin, the offer never came.

Special procedures are needed to allow scientists and engineers to maintain valuable professional contacts while protecting critical confidentiality. One good way is to establish a two-tier review process. In the first tier, a panel of the writer's peers reviews the material. If they approve its use in a forum outside the company, a second review is performed by company legal counsel. If counsel agrees that the matter is suitable for publication, a presentation approval is given.

Of course, rules for securing office computing also apply in the laboratory. Special or unusual computers that cannot be secured in line with company procedures must be protected on an exception basis according to company policy.

In some laboratories (for example, the Xerox Corporation paper physics laboratory in Toronto), both document security controls and references to materials are made easier by requiring that all documents be stored as microfilm or electronic images. Comparing a laboratory with electronic data storage with one in which paper is the medium—stacks of notebooks and piles of paper everywhere—is a real lesson in efficiency.

THE ENGINEERING FUNCTION

Engineering is a critical activity in high technology businesses. It might be said that engineering is where the competitive battles are won. Engineering activity creates and uses a great deal of high-value, sensitive information. Careful attention is required to proper identification, classification, handling, marking, and storage of information in the form of plans, drawings, and notebooks.

Company legal counsel should be consulted to determine the appropriate proprietary markings for engineering documents. In many instances, engineering materials should be marked both with the company information classification and with a legal notice of rights, such as the following:

> This document contains unpublished proprietary information which is the property of ABCompany. Copyright 1995 by ABCompany. All rights reserved.

Engineering notebooks should be carefully maintained in a form and composition specified by the company. These notebooks should be numbered and controlled and always remain company property. They could be important should a lawsuit involve proprietary rights to information concerning the matters described in the notebooks.

Computer-aided design (CAD) equipment requires security protection for files and drawings that may be stored on-line or in disk or tape storage. Any files that contain valuable or irreplaceable materials should be copied and then stored securely at a remote site.

Case

XYZ Company had spent $500,000 in the development of a new product. The drawings for the product were stored in paper files and on a CAD computer disk, all within one engineering area. A fire destroyed the plans and the computer. The company lost the investment, because all the relative documentation was in one place.

MANUFACTURING

Microcomputers have become commonplace in manufacturing operations. They are used for reporting on work in progress, raw material and component quality check results, employee time and attendance, materials and parts requisitions, stockroom management, and other such matters. Although most of these activities are routine, information security remains an important consideration. The small data centers in manufacturing facilities where terminal or workstation inputs are processed should be protected in the same way as any other data-processing facility. In some cases, the manufacturing site may be a risky environment, and contingency recovery plans are essential.

FIELD OFFICES

Field offices are often out of sight, out of mind, and employees in small, remote locations may not have the awareness or motivation to institute information security measures. Because many of these offices may have direct interface with the company's customers, it is very important that special effort be made to establish information security practices and accountability. Employees who do not know or care about information protection can be the weak link in the chain that allows sensitive competitive information to escape.

Case

A marketing employee resigned from the ICHH company. Although she had given notice to ICHH, she requested and was issued a current list of prospective customers and their anticipated product needs. Later, ICHH discovered that several customers had switched suppliers. These customers were on that prospects list.

RETAIL STORES

Most retail activities direct their security efforts toward physical security matters such as shoplifting, employee theft or fraud, and merchandise shortages. However, as with field offices, an employee who does not know about information protection may turn out to be the cause of a serious loss.

WORKING AT HOME AND AWAY

Many executives and knowledge workers have computing and communication resources that allow them to do company work at home, in hotel rooms, at airports, and even in automobiles or airplanes. The provision of portable, individualized computing power is a boon to workers who must spend a great deal of time traveling. It also allows employees who may have valid reasons for working at home—such as personal or family illness, transportation problems, weather emergencies, excessive workloads, caring for children—to be productive in circumstances that would otherwise be considered lost time.

As with any computer or network access, this portable personal access phenomenon carries with it severe security vulnerabilities. Several advanced and reliable systems are available for authentication of users at unpredictable locations. These include smartcards, microprocessors embedded in plastic cards, that work alone or with operating system or telephone system features to establish reliable authentication.

The ubiquitous password, however, remains the most commonly used method for proving identity with portable or remote access, primarily because of the costs involved with more robust means of authentication.

Some of the risks associated with portable personal access are as follows:

- Unauthorized observation of access-control processes or sensitive information when the user is in an environment where privacy is difficult. For example, people working in an airliner seat can hardly assume that material entered to a laptop computer (perhaps for later transmission through a company network) can be private.
- Use of a public telephone or microcomputer in an airline club may introduce vulnerabilities. Such public systems may contain unknown code, introduced by other casual users, which may have hidden purposes. Although no specific cases are at hand, it seems that airline club computers are a likely source of virus software. This is a real and serious vulnerability for anyone who uses these publicly available computers.

Case

An executive used a laptop computer and a public telephone at an airport to transmit a customer proposal. For convenience he wrote the access codes on top of the proposal preparation form. When he completed the transmission, the executive gathered his papers but forgot the proposal form. In an amazing stroke of fortune, another employee of the company came along and found the form. In most cases such good fortune does not occur.

- Working at home introduces another set of risks. Family members may be told about or may observe an employee's access procedures. If family members also use the company-provided computer or terminal—the predominant situation—there is a risk that data may be polluted or exposed.

Case

An executive working at home allowed a teenage child to watch the access process. The teenager then provided the sign-on procedures to her high school computer class. An access at the school resulted in exposure of highly sensitive information and the threat of a lawsuit.

Case

An employee working at home printed several iterations of a sensitive company strategic plan he was developing. Later, his wife retrieved the paper from a wastebasket and provided it to a nursery school as drawing paper. Some children in the class carried the material home, where it was recognized by an employee of a competitor. The material was eventually returned to its owner, but exposure had to be assumed.

When sensitive information is developed or used within a company's facilities, one can assume a certain level of protection. This does not hold true once the information leaves the company premises. Many cases of losses of sensitive information because people were careless outside the office have been reported.

Case

Executives working on an airplane left behind the company's annual strategic plan. A manager from a competing company discovered the document. It was returned to the originator with assurances that it had not been read.

USE OF COMPUTERS WHEN TRAVELING

Information should be protected in all its forms (mental, written, electronic). Both paper and electronic forms may be at risk when one uses computers in unfamiliar surroundings.

Today most computing involves connection with telecommunications networks, which offer efficiency and economy. However, electronic information is at risk whenever it is transmitted over networks. Data communications facilities invariably pass through switching centers where government technicians or others can easily observe and record messages or documents. Clandestine eavesdropping by means of local tapping of telephone lines is absurdly simple and easy.

Using a personal computer in a hotel that provides computer network connection poses substantial possibility of exposure. The following precautions are recommended as minimal steps for information protection:

- Carefully consider the risks versus the benefits of using electronic mail. Always assume that a private exchange of information is unlikely.
- When possible, encrypt sensitive information. If encryption is impractical, use code. Agree beforehand (perhaps by a telephone call from a location other than the one from which the computer is to be used) with the recipient of the message that you will substitute certain words on a one-time basis.

- Lock all floppy disks and documents containing sensitive information in your brief-case and carry it with you whenever you are not in your hotel room, even if you are only going to dinner in the hotel.
- If you use an impact printer, consider the printer ribbon to be a document and dispose of it carefully when you finish printing.
- Beware of facsimile machines. Fax transmissions are notorious for information leaks, especially at the receiving end, where output is often available to passers-by.

Using Floppy Disks

Business people frequently carry floppy disks for use in computers provided by hotels, business partners, office services providers, and others. There are two evident risks.

First, the computer itself may be infected with virus software code. This code could cause copies of your files and messages to be secretly made or sent to others. The virus could also cause immediate or delayed damage to your files or programs.

Second, the computer's hard disk may retain information you enter for processing or temporary storage, even after you have erased it. The ERASE command does not really delete information; it only removes the pointers used by the system to find files. Software is available that can allow other users to clandestinely read erased information.

Suggested precautions are as follows:

- Carry two copies of any important disks; keep one as a back-up in case one is damaged. If unusual displays or sequences of operation occur, or if processing seems unusually slow, stop work and obtain another computer. These unusual displays or delays may be symptoms of the presence of a software virus. Do not try another disk.
- Your company security manager may be able to recommend a virus protection package to be run before you begin work on an unfamiliar computer; it is a good idea to run such a program. However, no protection method is proof against all the new viruses continually introduced.
- Do not use disks provided by anyone you do not know well and trust. Be especially wary of disks with games or utility programs. These are most likely to have virus software on them.
- If you must use a computer's hard disk, obtain a program that overwrites the data on the disk and use it when you are finished working—after making copies of important files on your own new floppy disks.

International Business

Office managers responsible for business operations outside the country should establish precautionary measures that recognize that risks may be different or more severe in societies that may have different ethical standards. In general, a higher level of security awareness and precaution is appropriate.

CHECKLIST

The following is a checklist for prudent office computing:

- All employees turn off (sign-off) computers when they will be away from their workstations for more than some set period of time, as prudent and appropriate. Thirty minutes is suggested.
- All floppy disks are locked away when not in use, as are the documents they contain.
- Employees' personal disks—with games or utilities—are never brought to the office. No personal work is performed on office computers.
- Employees authorized to work at home never intermingle business computing with personal computing. Only business programs are run on company machines provided for home use. Personal programs or data are never loaded on company computers.
- Home-to-office network communication is carefully defined and limited to approved business.
- All workstations have effective security at sign-on; this usually means that the employee must have a key (to switch on power) or a password (to boot).
- Employees are trained and security-conscious. They select strong passwords (at least eight characters, difficult to guess, not in English or local dictionary) and keep them secret.
- Outsiders are not allowed in office areas where sensitive information may be displayed or is at hand on desks or workstations in documents or disks.

SUMMARY

Information protection is always a matter of paying attention to detail. Business managers must be aware and alert. Casual, careless use of information eventually results in its loss or exposure.

NOTES

1. *MIS Week*, April 9, 1990.
2. S. L. Berry, *Management Review*, July 1990.
3. *Wall Street Journal*, December 10, 1989.
4. *Newsweek*, European edition, July 31, 1989.

8

Computer Security

Computer security is addressed at some length in the previous chapter, since computers are integral parts of almost all business environments. However, computers are undoubtedly the principal means for processing, storing, and communicating information in the 1990s. They also present the most severe vulnerability to a company's information. In this chapter more detail is provided for those whose primary interest is in securing computers. In its landmark report, *Computers at Risk* (1991), the United States National Research Council suggested ten system security principles. These principles are as follows:[1]

1. *Quality control.* A system must be trusted to do what is expected to do and only that. Independent analysis and evaluation of system components (software, hardware, procedures) and their correctness and reliability are needed. This principle implies that a formal installation process include careful review and testing of the system for security, integrity, and reliability. Traditionally, such testing has been narrowly focused on software correctness; this is important but needs to be broadened in scope.

2. *Access control for program code as well as for data.* Controls should define which actions are allowed to specified users, in addition to specifying which users may access which data. (A *user* can be a program as well as a person.)

3. *User identification and authentication.* Every system must be able to reliably identify each user claiming access rights. Emphasis on passwords as means of authentication must be supplemented with stronger proofs, such as those offered by the use of smartcards or encryption-based authentication.

4. *Protection of executable code.* A process must be in place to control modification of software in application programs and in operating systems. This process implies a means for management control over such changes and an assurance that the appropriate quality checks have been performed before the changes are implemented. This is an illustration of one of many critical procedural elements.

5. *Security logging.* All security-relevant events that occur during system operation must be recorded for later study and analysis. The logging process must be protected against attack. Certain particularly dangerous situations should result in immediate activation of alarms and self-protecting processes, perhaps by means of artificial intelligence methods.

6. *Security administration.* Certain users must have the necessary privileges and responsibilities to take any action necessary to protect the system. These responsibilities include modification of the rights and privileges of other users, control of software, and preparation for emergency management and recovery.

7. *Data encryption.* Encryption provides the only reliable method for protecting data in communication systems.
8. *Operational support tools.* The security administrator requires tools that enable inspection and verification of the security status of the system. Typically these tools are special software constructs that monitor important system elements.
9. *Independent audit.* Just as in other business operations, the computer system should be subject to surprise audits to verify that the system is in control and that the other computer security principles are being observed.
10. *Hazard analysis.* An effort is made to identify and describe what can go wrong, so that appropriate protective measures may be adopted. This is a forward look or risk analysis process.

HOW COMPUTER SECURITY RELATES TO INFORMATION SECURITY

Computer security is one of the components of information security (see Table 4.1). For our purposes, *computer security* includes telecommunications security and network security. These activities use computers as switching machines, database stores, servers, and processors; hence, proper computer security cover is all-inclusive.

As often used, the term *computer security* is actually a misnomer. In the days when hardware was extremely expensive and scarce, preservation of the machines was important. Strangely, those were the days of the glass-house data center. Today, hardware is relatively inexpensive, and the real value is in the information being processed and stored and in the application software. The situation is similar to that in a jewelry store; one does not worry about the display cabinets or the building. The computers are containers for the valuable, irreplaceable asset called *information.*

Computer security has the same three levels of protective elements as information security. The levels are as follows:

- Physical security
- Procedural or administrative security
- Logical or hardware-software security

PHYSICAL SECURITY FOR COMPUTING

Physical security consists of the guards, door locks and physical access-control systems, traps, vaults, specially secured areas, closed-circuit television and proximity detection systems, fire control systems, and other methods for the management of physical space. In general, physical security for computers has the two following purposes:

- To provide protection for and control over access to computers
- To provide for the secure storage of computer media and output

Physical security for areas that contain sensitive operations such as a data center or laboratory usually requires implementing physical access controls, which enforce specific personal authorizations. Access can be controlled with magnetic-card identifier systems, hand geometry, physical recognition, or similar methods to restrict entry.

Also required are fire alarm and suppression systems and procedures to protect against water damage. Most serious losses of computing services and stored or on-line data occur as a result of fire and subsequent extinguishing efforts.

Case

A data center in a basement of a building in Milan, Italy, was severely damaged after a fire on the seventh floor. Although the fire was localized and did not go beyond the floor where it originated, thousands of gallons of water poured into the structure, flowed down a stairwell and through openings in ceilings and floors, and eventually flooded the basement.

Physical shielding—to prevent emanations from computer equipment—may be required in circumstances where extremely valuable or sensitive information is processed. (Emanations control is called Tempest by the U.S. military.) Demonstrations have shown that emanations are relatively easy to pick up in many circumstances. But because of the difficulties in separating signals and in selection of desired data, such shielding is not considered essential for most business applications.

In today's distributed business systems environment, where access to computers—and the information they hold—is more likely to be logical than physical, physical security measures are fairly generalized and localized. That is, the data center has stringent physical security measures custom-designed for the purpose. Microcomputers and terminals in the offices and engineering and manufacturing areas depend largely on logical security measures for protection against unauthorized use.

Information system managers and information security managers should rely on the advice of the company's professional security experts in making decisions about physical security for computers. There is a common misunderstanding about the relative roles of the physical-security experts and the information-security experts. Knowing about computing and information science may enable someone to make suitable decisions about logical protection, but being an expert in computing does not make one an expert in physical security.

PROCEDURAL AND ADMINISTRATIVE SECURITY

Hackers and wiretaps are glamorous and intriguing. But security depends on a series of critical but tedious administrative procedures. Paying attention to detail results in reliable and consistent information protection. In many cases, extremely clever and perhaps expensive logical security measures involving access-control software and hardware mechanisms are compromised because those responsible failed to pay attention to the mundane administrative details.

Important administrative and procedural matters essential to computer security include the following:

- Proper classification of company information on computers, which allows the most suitable and effective computer security measures to be applied.
- Identification and authorization of employees allowed to see, modify, or move specific data files and the maintenance of this information currently with business requirements and employee job assignments. The decision that authorizes employees, contractors, suppliers, or customers to access certain company information files usually is made by the information owner. The decision should never be made by information system or computer operations people.
- Monitoring of security-related events during computer processing. This activity includes the identification of events that may be considered threats and the investigation and analysis of such events. In most cases, mainframe computers can spew out such a plethora of security data that even the most dedicated security managers throw up their hands in dismay. Hence some form of data reduction is a necessity. Nevertheless, daily review of the data is important.
- Monitoring of computer users' prudence and compliance with established company computer security directives. Prudence involves users' selection of passwords. The company's security standards may require an eight- or twelve-position password; the employees may decide that names provide an easy way to comply with the requirement. For example, "Richard J. Smith" includes alpha and special characters and exceeds twelve positions, but if *Richard J. Smith* is the user's name, this is not a prudent password. Much of the monitoring can be performed with security software, but in some cases, administrative intervention might be necessary.
- Processes for intervention when user problems occur. An illustration is forgetting a password. A person in authority must be able to help the user resume his or her work. Another illustration involves the loss of an authentication token such as a smartcard. Someone in authority must cancel the lost token and issue a new one.
- Management of software and hardware security tools. This activity addresses the administrative and control processes involved in using security packages such as IBM's RACF (Resources Access Control Facility), Digital's INSPECT (Interactive Network Security Policy Examination/Compliance Toolset), and similar software. Part of this work involves the monitoring activities described earlier; part of it has to do with installing and using the tools.
- Administration of encryption keys and the authorizations to possess those keys. In some encryption services, keys must be changed in tightly controlled circumstances.
- Management of the operations environment. Typically this activity is part of the system quality control process. It involves monitoring activities by privileged users (i.e., those who have special rights relating to activities such as software maintenance and hardware maintenance), monitoring vendor engineering and maintenance support activities, and controlling updates to software libraries.

Case

All data centers of a worldwide company were warned that computer hackers had attacked certain computers when the default password, set by the manufacturer at time of delivery, was not changed at computer installation. In spite of these warnings, one data center reported an attack with the same cause. A blasé attitude about a simple precaution caused the loss of a resource.

LOGICAL SECURITY

Strict procedures for access to the machine room are used by most organizations, and these procedures are often an organization's only obvious computer security measures. Today, however, with pervasive remote terminal access, communications, and networking, physical measures rarely provide meaningful protection for either the information or the service; only the hardware is secure. Nonetheless, most computer facilities continue to protect their physical machines far better than they do their data, even when the value of the data is several times greater than the value of the hardware.[2]

Logical security processes should eventually replace most physical and administrative security procedures and methods. Artificial intelligence–based processes combined with strong authentication methods should or could eliminate many of the administrative burdens now necessary for effective computer security. Although research has and is being conducted and although unit costs are coming down, the cost of an advanced security system continues to make us reliant on older, less reliable computer security controls.

Logical security systems typically consist of software programs, hardware assemblies, or combinations of both. There are three broad types of logical security systems. The three types are as follows:

- Systems that deal with the problems of identifying and authenticating users and programs that attempt to access computer resources or information. These are *logical security access-control systems.*
- Systems that deal with problems involving the integrity, reliability, and security of computer hardware, networks, and processing activities involved in operations. These are *environmental-control systems.*
- Systems that protect against eavesdropping or observation of sensitive data in transmission or in storage. These are *information assurance systems.*

Access-Control Systems

Three basic processes are involved in the operation of logical access-control systems—identification, authentication, and authorization.

Identification   The system first examines an identity claim, or token, presented by the user or program. For access-control purposes, a computer program, which may be acting as the agent of a human, can be considered a user and is required to submit to the same control processes as human users. This identity claim might be an employee name or identifier typed into the computer from a keyboard. It also might be a number or word read from a magnetic strip on a plastic identity card. Or it might be a program name affixed to a header label written into the instructions in a program.

In any case, the access-control system of a computer tries to match the claimed identity against an established list of identities. If a match is made, the system proceeds with an authentication attempt, described later. If no match is made, the user or program is refused further service or, more typically, is asked to try again.

The matter of trying again is key to effective protection. Even small delays in servicing subsequent attempts place a severe burden on a hacker attempting a break-in. Unlimited attempts at any stage of access control should never be allowed. After two or three unsuccessful tries, the system should send an alarm and shut off further attempts.

Authentication   The access-control system requires the user or program attempting a connection to provide proof of the claimed and recognized identity. As an illustration of authentication, consider that you are called to the telephone and a voice at the other end says "Dad, this is your son Paul!" but the line is so poor that you cannot recognize his voice. You would probably want to talk for a minute to try to recognize him through other means, for example, by his diction, inflection, and knowledge of family affairs. These additional proofs of claimed identity can be considered authentication tokens. Once you accept the tokens you know that it is your son Paul. Similarly, although the access-control system recognizes the claimant as an identified user or program when the identifier is successfully matched, the user's identity is not proved until an authentication token is matched with both the identifier and a list of authenticators.

Within the access-control system is an authentication list, which may be called by other names but generally consists of a related series of data in the format

USER/PROGRAM NAME—IDENTIFIER—AUTHENTICATOR—
AUTHORIZATION

Table 8–1 illustrates such a file.

In the authentication process, the access-control system determines that the accepted identifier and the offered authenticator match.

The authenticator should be a token with relatively strong security. In most cases, this is a secret password. Other, more reliable tokens may include a smartcard, hand geometry, a retinal scan, a fingerprint, a voice print, or a signature. In these cases the

Table 8–1   Access Control List

User/Program Name	Identifier	Authenticator	Authorization
David Smith	EC2134	Exrayvision	A2139
Chris Jones	M08733	AkronOhio21674	AM7805
Payroll799	payroll	&511Z7009	AMDpayroll

measured physical (or biometric) data are converted to digital format and matched against the stored authentication token.

If the authentication match is successful, the user or program is considered genuine. However, the fact that the access-control system accepts the identity of the user or program as genuine does not imply a right or privilege to see, use, or modify the information. Hence, the authorization step is required.

Passwords

The most commonly used means for authenticating computer users, and unfortunately the weakest, is the password. However, although the password has many deficiencies as an authentication token, it has one important advantage: Passwords are inexpensive and easy to use. Smartcards, retinal scans, voice prints, fingerprints, and combinations of biometric measures or physical tokens with passwords offer far greater reliability and security, but they are expensive. Except for high-risk situations, the cost of alternative methods means that the password will remain the principal means of user authentication for some time to come.

There are generally agreed rules concerning password use. Carefully observing these rules makes it fairly certain that unauthorized parties will not be able to sign on to or otherwise access office computers, files, or mainframe computers connected to the office by means of networks.

Prudent passwords have the following qualities.

- Contain at least eight characters
- Mix alphabetic, numeric, and special characters
- Cannot be found in a dictionary (modern hacker techniques use dictionary word lists to search quickly for matches with passwords)
- Are kept secret by the user
- Are changed periodically to new and different words/phrases (Old passwords eventually become exposed.) A password's effectiveness is measured by its "safe time." That is the time it would take an attacker to succeed in guessing or matching the password. The safe time depends on the following:

    1. The transmission rate of characters being exchanged between attacker and computer. Security can extend this rate of exchange by causing a delay after each failed attempt.
    2. The number of characters exchanged in any one log-on attempt. Each character tried adds a few microseconds to the attacker's workload.
    3. The minimum number of characters in the passwords used. More characters increase the population of passwords in use. Increasing the number of passwords greatly increases the time required (or the computing power required) for guessing or matching. Eight characters are considered adequate if the next rule is followed.
    4. The number of characters in the available set used for passwords. A four-character password using alphabet only gives 456,976 possibilities. Extending the set to include numerals increases the possibilities to 1,679,616. Passwords that include only alphabetic characters are weaker than passwords that consist of all usable computer characters.

Authorization   The access-control system must determine that the identified and authenticated user is authorized to perform specific actions and must limit the user or program to the established privileges. In Table 8–1, the authorization entries show *A*, *M*, and *D*. These codes mean *access*, *modify*, and *delete*. These are privileges granted to individual employees or programs, or to groups of employees or programs, by the information owner or information custodian. Some employees may be allowed only to see certain data entries, whereas others may be allowed to modify or delete information. This authorization process relates to the need-to-know rule, which is the basis for information integrity. In other words, information can be believed (has integrity) because only parties authorized to do so can make modifications.

Access-control Implementations

Access-control systems are implemented in different ways depending on the architecture of the particular computer operating system. In general, security for IBM computers is provided by adding special security software packages. These programs interface with the operating system. Examples of such packages include:

> For IBM MVS and VM—RACF, CA-ACF-2, CA-Top Secret
>
> For IBM MS-DOS—Watchdog, PC Watchman, Privacy Plus, OnGuard, MicroLock

Digital Equipment Corporation's VMS operating system has access-control software built in. The user must determine the appropriate security policy and then make the correct adjustments and settings. Other computer manufacturers offer similar arrangements. There are advantages and disadvantages to either approach (Table 8–2).

ENVIRONMENTAL-CONTROL SYSTEMS

> *Security is a complex property and difficult to design or optimize. Designing a system to be efficient, convenient or cheap is an optimization problem which, though complex in practice, has a mathematical structure which is easy to understand . . . [but] designing a system for security means analyzing an adversary problem where the designer and the opponents are each thinking out their strategies.*
>
> D.W. Davies and W.L. Price, *Security for Computer Networks* (New York: John Wiley & Sons, 1987), 3.

Environmental control is a complex subject. This book does not attempt to discuss it in detail but does provide some introduction and explanation. Computer environmental-control systems consist of various hardware arrangements and software programs,

Table 8–2   Added-on versus Integral Access-control Software

Type of Software	Advantages	Disadvantages
Added-on	Simple administration	Added cost
	Separation of duties	Complex interaction among programs
Integral	Potentially more rigorous security	No added costs
		Technicians must administer

which are usually within the operating system. Among other things, these systems do the following:

- Ensure separation of user or program spaces within the computer's memory. This is important to provide integrity of process. It is critical that one user not be able to move into a space occupied by another user or another user's data. This is usually a hardware-implemented function.
- Protect the operations and data transfers within the computer processes from improper access or interference. This may be implemented in hardware or software or both.
- Monitor the correctness and security of the computer environment. These functions are often provided by external software constructs called *tools*.

For an excellent explanation of the detail of such processes within the operating system, see Gasser's *Building a Secure Computer System* (Van Nostrand Reinhold, 1988).

COMPUTER SECURITY TOOLS

Computer and network security tools are being developed, often with artificial intelligence, to provide services for real-time monitoring and control of the computing environment. These tools fall into the following five general categories:[3]

1. *Local node policy violation and correction.* Such tools assure that local system management has complied with company security standards, and if not, can take action to remedy the situation. Some of these tools provide a lock-down of the computer; in other words, the tool forces the system into compliance.
2. *Remote security checking.* This tool allows a security manager at a central site to contact and inspect the security status of a remote computer.
3. *Intrusion detection and countermeasures.* This kind of tool usually applies artificial intelligence or computer learning to detect suspicious or dangerous events, make records, and in real time establish defensive action, such as shutting off an attacker or disconnecting a threatening entity.

4. *Audit data reduction and analysis.* These tools collect the many bits of data from monitoring systems and sort the data into a more convenient form, allowing recognition of important security events.
5. *Integrity assurance.* This tool checks for the integrity of various objects such as files, queues, and system generation parameters.

The second type of tool listed, remote security violation analysis, is intended for management use in checking behavior. The other tools are for security managers and system operators.

INFORMATION ASSURANCE SYSTEMS

Cryptography is an ancient science. The word means *secret writing.* The application of cryptography to computing (or more properly information protection) is usually called *encryption,* meaning the conversion of information, by means of a mathematical algorithm, to a nonrepetitive cipher. Cryptography is used to protect against several computer-related information threats. Most of these threats involve networks, but encryption is a computer process. Threats that justify the use of encryption include the following:

- Eavesdropping on communications lines or radio transmissions
- Reading of sensitive files stored on disk or tape
- Collection of data from emanations
- Clandestine modification of messages

Cryptography also offers a means to sign or prove the authenticity of files or messages or forms. In a simplified illustration, a message or file is converted to a cipher by means of processing the original (or clear-text) message against a key (a code or set of characters) with an algorithm (a set of rules or processing steps). When the message is delivered, the recipient must have the same key and must process the cipher received through the inverse process. The clear text (human-readable message) then appears. Encryption and decryption can be accomplished manually (at great effort) or, as in almost all cases today, through software programs or special hardware.

The algorithm used for encryption is not necessarily secret. The key is always secret. Having the key is the same as having the information. So the key must be protected at the same level as the information; in other words, a message classified as *ABCompany Registered* must be protected by a key classified as *ABCompany Registered* and handled accordingly.

It must be assumed that any security barrier can be breached given enough time, effort, and resources. A *work factor* is the amount of time and effort needed to break down protection. As with passwords, an effective encryption process presents a would-be attacker with a work factor too great to justify the effort. Depending on the value and useful life of the information sought, an effective encryption process is one that does the following:

- Has an algorithm of sufficient complexity that it is not reasonably possible to develop the key by analysis
- Provides sufficient protection so that an attack by means of key exhaustion (trying to develop all possible keys) or statistical method (using powerful computers) would produce results that would be too late for or too expensive for the attacker's purpose

This book does not provide sufficient detail concerning encryption methods and complexities to allow good decisions on the application of encryption to a given circumstance. See Davies and Price's *Security for Computer Networks* (John Wiley & Sons, 1987) for in-depth discussion.

PRACTICAL PROCEDURES FOR COMPUTER SECURITY

The explanations and procedures described are based on computer security standards developed at Xerox Corporation and at Digital Equipment Corporation. They are presented in generic form and could be used in almost any business.

Managing Computer Accounts

Computer accounts are authorizations or approvals to use computer resources. Usually, such an account is granted for use of network-connected services and files. Procedures must ensure that all computer accounts are properly authorized, based on business requirements. Good management also requires that such accounts be maintained to ensure currency with assigned employee responsibilities. Account revalidation is required, or automatic account downgrading or disabling may be appropriate, as explained later.

A business, through management policy, must assign authority to establish computer accounts for employees. Managers are therefore responsible for managing the use of company computer accounts, or resources. Accounts should be managed in the context of local procedures. The size or geographic spread of a company may justify procedures established by local system or security managers. An essential player in such management is the company human resources department.

Local managers must be held responsible for making prompt deletions or changes to the authorized-user list when personnel actions such as termination, transfer, or job change so indicate. Information leading to such actions usually originates in the human resources department.

Privileged Accounts   Accounts with privileges (authority to perform controlled actions, such as loading operating-system software or modifying security software) are an important source of security vulnerability. The following special constraints should apply to accounts with privileges.

1. Privileged accounts must be given only to a single user and must never be shared by more than one user.

2. To ensure that accounts with privileges do not share an environment with a non-privileged account, business managers must check each account with privilege periodically to ensure the following:

    -   The privileged account does not share a user identifier with a nonprivileged account
    -   Any control processes managed are not shared with nonprivileged accounts

3. Any privileges required must be limited to the minimum rights needed.
4. Proxy access (authority shared with another person or entity) to a privileged account must not be allowed.
5. Accounts with privileges must not be used for routine work. In other words, a system maintenance programmer with privileges should not use the assigned system maintenance account for correspondence, writing application programs, or sending messages.

Routine Nonprivileged Accounts   All accounts must be restricted to the use dictated by formally assigned business-related responsibilities. Remote access by means of dial-up or direct connection with the company network should be only for exceptional cases. Businesses frequently use dial-up casually as a communication method; this does not make the practice a safe one.

Creating and Deleting Accounts   Corporate and local business managers must be advised of personnel changes that affect privileges. Company human resources managers must accept responsibility for such notification. These notifications should be formally established so as to ensure timeliness.

Creating Accounts with Privileges   Unauthorized access to accounts with privileges presents a critical risk to the security of systems and the information they contain. Positive, proactive management and control are essential. Accounts with privileges must be granted only by exception as justified by job assignment.

Accounts with privileges must provide the employee only privileges necessary to perform assigned business tasks. When practical, alternative means (e.g., access without privilege) should be pursued for accomplishing the assigned tasks. The following are guidelines for establishing privileged accounts:

1. A request for a privileged account should be in written form, following established company format and process. Such a request must clearly specify the privileges needed and must provide business justification in each case.
2. The application for privilege should require written approval by the authorizing business manager.
3. Records of the documents involved must be retained by the authorizing manager to allow auditing.
4. The information system organization responsible for maintaining the system or networks must concur with the request.

5. Account identifiers (user names or user identifiers) on a system must be unique. In other words, every account identifier must be different from every other. In the optimal situation, no two identifiers across the entire company would ever be the same. This is so because prudent control requires that the specific employee or contractor performing an action be held responsible.

Accounts without Privileges   Unauthorized access to nonprivileged accounts presents a risk to the security of the information contained within the account. Guidelines are as follows:

1. A request for an account without privileges may be accomplished in any practical manner appropriate for business needs and the maintenance of accountability.
2. Documents or other records must be retained by the authorizing manager as an auditable record.
3. The request must have the approval of the organization responsible for the related computer services.

Adding Privileges to an Account   An employee with a computer account may need to add privileged actions to routine actions already authorized. In such a case, requests for adding privileges to a nonprivileged account should follow a process substantially the same as that suggested for creating accounts with privileges.

Revalidating or Renewing Accounts   The purpose of revalidating accounts is to ensure that the user's authorization to access information or software remains valid and consistent with business purposes. An ongoing and current effort among security managers, system managers, and human resources managers in keeping accounts up-to-date facilitates local audit of accounts.

Revalidating Accounts with Privileges   Accounts with privileges should be revalidated periodically as appropriate for business circumstances or perceived risk. Revalidation should use paper forms to record the process and approval necessary. The authorized approving manager must question whether the privileges granted to the employee are still required. Automatic renewal of privilege is an invitation to fraud, mischief, and loss of control. Use of computers by employees no longer authorized such use is a frequent cause of mischief and loss.

Revalidating Accounts without Privileges   Revalidation of nonprivileged accounts should be performed to allow periodic revalidation of such actions. Revalidation must be approved by the authorizing manager.

Disabling or Suspending Accounts   Accounts not regularly used for business purposes that remain authorized pose a serious security threat and are a waste of resources. Disablement of an account should be based on a company-defined period of inactivity and the type of access. A lack of activity on an account should always be primary evidence that the account is not needed. No employee has an inherent right to the computer resources. Therefore, if account use is less than the company-set minimum, an account should be canceled.

Deletion or Cancellation of Accounts   Deletion of an account can be based on several factors, including period of inactivity, type of access, change in authorization, job change, transfer of employee to another site, or employee termination. Guidelines for deletion of accounts are as follows:

1. A list of deleted account identifiers must be retained, and identifiers should not be reused for at least one year to prevent inheritance of account rights by other employees and possible misdirection of electronic mail.
2. The responsible business manager must determine the disposition of the user's files when deleting an account. Depending on business circumstances, the appropriate action might be one of the following:

    - Delete files
    - Leave files in place
    - Save files that may be of use in future business (always a business decision, not a system decision)

3. Mail sent to the account after it is deleted or closed must be properly handled. Special care must be taken to ensure that company information is not automatically forwarded through automatic mail-forwarding systems to people no longer employed at the company.

Case

An employee at a research center was given leave of absence to attend a university. The employee arranged for electronic mail to be forwarded to the university network. When the scholastic term was completed, the employee chose to work for a different company. However, mail continued to be forwarded to the university, and sensitive research data were exposed to unauthorized people there.

Managing Accounts in Special Circumstances   Some situations require policy decisions and special handling. Company policies and the applicable local or national law covering the situation should provide specific guidance. Company policy should establish that employees or retirees do not have an inherent right to have a computer account on a company system. When business requirements dictate and appropriate management approves, such accounts may be provided as an exception.

Accounts for Nonemployees   In the modern international communications village, businesses often provide access to computer accounts for customers, suppliers, consultants, contractors, and other parties outside the company's formal organization. Each circumstance requires careful evaluation of the cultural, social, and business environment surrounding the situation. An early decision concerning prudent restrictions, to ensure continuing information security, is essential. This decision is best made if the company has set policy and procedure concerning review and approval of external access.

Outside sources exchanging electronic mail with a company should be required to access company networks through an established gateway. A service such as *X.400 Mail*, which is the worldwide standard, or similar service can provide effective control.

Managing Nonemployee Computer Access from Internal Locations   Any accounts provided for business reasons to customers, suppliers, consultants or contractors, or outside businesses that will be accessed from within a company facility require the usual access approval and review procedures. Guidelines are as follows:

1. Nonemployees should be provided with limited-access accounts.
2. Accounts provided to nonemployees should expire automatically upon termination of the contract.
3. The business manager responsible for the nonemployee's work must ensure that the nonemployee account expires properly.
4. The authorizing business manager should be held accountable for seeing that all company computer security standards are followed.
5. Following company policy, all nonemployees allowed to use company computer services should sign company information-disclosure agreements.

Managing Accounts Provided to Nonemployees for Access   The company should have an established process for reviewing and approving such access. The process—usually a management control over resource use—should include a careful review of the information security implications of the connection.

Managing Security of Computer Accounts

Accounts of different types and authorities call for different security requirements.

Account Identifiers   Each account must have a unique owner identified. In determining the forms of identification to be used, the security manager must provide a method to allow specific individual responsibility to be determined.

Application Software Accounts   If business computer applications (i.e., sets of program codes intended to accomplish a business purpose, such as a payroll system or a work-in-process system) require accounts, those accounts must not compromise account management. Application programs should never create accounts to be used for any kind of control. System or control actions must always be performed from an authorized, privileged account that is associated with an individual.

Software Development Accounts   Software development accounts do not automatically justify full privileges. Requirements for account creation established by the company should apply in such cases. All such accounts must be clearly associated with an individual through the account identifier.

System Maintenance Accounts   Access provided for computer engineers or field-services workers should be tightly controlled. Responsible managers should never assume that service technicians are to be blindly trusted. The access privileges provided should be the minimum needed, and they should expire for reevaluation on a regular basis.

Establishing Control of Access to Computer Resources

Effective security requires that individual users be identified, typically by a username or account name and subsequently authenticated by an authentication token (something the user is, has, or knows). The common token is a password, but stronger authentication may be provided with biometric devices. Proper use of passwords for user authentication requires effective password construction, password expiration, and maintenance of password confidentiality. Company password standards should provide rules for password use that meet the threats reasonably anticipated.

Password Construction   Employee-selected passwords must be constructed so as to resist guessing or testing. Passwords must not contain words found in the dictionary, personal or family names, or other terms readily associated with the employee. The following are never acceptable as passwords: location names, account names, account owner's name, employee's name, any items in list but read backward, or single dictionary words.

Good security results from passwords that combine alphabetic, numeric, and special characters, for example:

1229sixthstreet
oldmanriver

Password Length   Passwords for accounts that grant privileges should be at least 15 characters long. Passwords for other accounts should be eight characters long.

Protection of Passwords   A primary purpose of passwords is to establish responsibility for computer use. Passwords for all account types must be kept secret by the individual user, and in normal business situations, passwords must never be shared with others. However, because security does not run the business, extenuating circumstances may dictate that a password may be shared temporarily with another person. Sharing should be allowed only with specific approval by the responsible business manager. As soon as the need for sharing is ended, the password must be changed and again held secret to one person. In any case and without exception, the password holder should be held responsible for any and all actions taken by anyone to whom the password has been disclosed.

Employees should be encouraged to memorize passwords. When it is impractical to memorize, a password may be written down and carried in a wallet or purse (as one would protect a credit card) or locked in a desk. Passwords should never be displayed or kept where they may be casually observed.

Password Lifetime   When operating systems provide such features, the computer should force password expiration and provide user notification of the need for password renewal. When operating systems do not provide such features, equivalent end-of-life controls must be provided through methods or procedures. All passwords eventually become unreliable because of the probability of exposure. Therefore, all passwords should expire after a reasonable time, which is determined on the basis of business needs and perceived risks.

Reusing Passwords   Previously used passwords should not be reused, particularly on the same system or network. When the operating system provides password control features, appropriate time-limit settings for reuse should be required. Appropriate manual systems should be used as a control if the operating system does not support reuse limits.

Storing Passwords Securely   The computer system must always store passwords in a one-way encrypted file. Passwords must never be embedded in user-written sign-on utilities. For example, an unauthorized user must never be able to authenticate at sign-on by merely using a function key or by running an unprotected program. Operating-system access passwords must be encrypted in the computer files. Passwords must never be displayed, echoed, or printed by the system.

Changing Passwords   A routine password change should require the employee to demonstrate that he or she has possession of the old password before a change to a new password can be processed. A new account requires that a one-time password be provided to the employee. After initial sign-on, the system must require that the one-time password be immediately changed to one known only to the authorized user.

Delivery of Passwords to Users   The company must establish suitable procedures to maintain password secrecy in all circumstances that may arise, such as forgotten passwords, new passwords, or delivery or communication of first-time passwords. It is essential in all such cases that the person who issues the password, regardless of circumstance, has positive identification of the employee being provided the password.

Keeping Security Records

All events that appear to affect security must be recorded for possible investigation. Events that should be automatically logged by the operating system include failures in attempted sign-in, attempts to break into the system by testing passwords or other evident questionable actions, failures when attempting access to files, accesses to operating system files, and any modification of authorizations or establishment of new accounts.

Certain incidents call for action beyond logging. These include any attempt to modify or delete authentication or authorization files, audit or accounting files, or password dictionary or password history files.

Data center managers or system managers should have established procedures for frequent review of all system messages, and operators should be trained in emergency reaction procedures to respond to system alarm notifications.

Monitoring and Analysis

Company security managers should establish procedures for auditing, system surveillance, and reporting of security incidents as locally devised. Computer center and system managers should have established procedures for shutting down systems or disconnecting systems from networks if such action is appropriate in specified security emergencies (for example, an ongoing and unresolved network attack from outside the company). The assigned business manager is responsible for ensuring that all required computer security tools are used and that security reports are properly prepared, reviewed, and forwarded as specified by company policy.

Managing Emergencies

Business managers at all levels should be held accountable for ensuring that local computer system emergency processes are set up and all necessary employees trained. Company business divisions, units, and locations must be provided with specific emergency procedures and procedures for reporting network and computer security violations.

Computer System Updates

Responsible business managers must work with supporting system organizations to ensure that security software releases or patches are installed promptly. This is essential because security fixes often follow findings of weakness or attacks experienced elsewhere. On any access to a company's internal network and systems, computer screens should display a warning to the effect that the computer is private property and is not available for public or unauthorized use.

Securing Personal Computing

Personal computers are commonplace and have become the generally accepted means for accomplishing knowledge work. However, personal computers present unique and serious security vulnerabilities. Personal computers include desktop personal computing systems, systems used at home or while traveling, portable (laptop or notebook) computing systems, workstations, and similar systems.

Company business managers who authorize the use of personal computers for business should be responsible for proper security training and awareness of employees who use such computers.

Company security managers should be held responsible for establishing appropriate personal computing security procedures, including appropriate company property control to ensure the security of portable computing equipment.

Company employees who use personal computers at home, while traveling, or at the workplace for company business purposes have the information security responsibility to protect company information from unauthorized exposure, loss of integrity, damage, or destruction. Employee users of personal computers also are responsible for protection of systems and devices, data media, and documents.

Business managers, security managers, and users of personal computers should be assigned specific information security responsibilities. The company must establish security awareness training programs for users of personal computers and reinforce the training at regular intervals. The company also must establish procedures for user reporting of security-related problems and for prompt handling and resolution of such problems; periodic audits or reviews of users of personal computers; and effective emergency reaction procedures to deal with incidents or suspicions reported by users of personal computers.

Software used or stored on personal computers for company business must meet the following quality standards:

- The software must have been obtained from an authorized company source.
- The software must have been obtained through the established company purchasing procedures in a sealed package from a supplier that licenses such products for the company's use.
- The software must have been thoroughly tested to ensure quality and reliability. For example, the package must be run on a stand-alone computer for several complete cycles or for an extended time to allow validation of program processes and output against the specifications provided.
- The software source code must have been examined to determine any obvious problems, or the code must have been verified as one of proved reliability.

Software obtained from a computer bulletin board or free software exchange or that is a home product prepared by an individual poses severe security risks. Such software is often a carrier of software viruses. The company should establish clear policy and control to prevent use of such software in business situations or on any personal computer used at any time for company business. The company should provide convenient facilities for scanning disks that contain software intended for loading on personal computers for use in company business.

System Integrity Employees who use personal computers should be required to meet reasonable standards of system integrity. These might include the following:

- Never intermingle approved company software with unapproved, untested software (for example, bulletin board, shareware, public domain software) on a system used for company business purposes.
- Never use a company-provided system for personal or other purposes not approved by the responsible business manager.

Physical Protection   Personal computers are used in the home, while traveling, at customer sites, in airport clubs, and even in public telephone booths. In every case, the employee must be made responsible for protection of the company's information and computing devices. Documents that contain the company's business information, whether or not classified, are to be protected from casual observation. Documents, floppy disks, tapes, or other media that contain company classified information must be locked away when not in use. *Locked away* means placed in a locked desk, file cabinet, safe, briefcase, or suitcase. When an employee works at home, such materials must be locked in a suitable receptacle. The company should provide employees with secure document storage (for example, a locking file cabinet or equivalent). Business managers should establish property controls to allow control and inventory of company-provided personal computers.

Logical Security   Users of personal computers should be provided with security software appropriate for protection of information. At a minimum, the employee should be able to apply protection measures robust enough to prevent access to data by use of commonly available computer programs. The security measures provided to the employee must allow sufficient protection so that a thief or penetrator is forced to use unacceptably expensive or difficult means to penetrate to company data.

The personal computer access-control process must deny sign-on or boot unless the user has a necessary password or other authenticating token or a physical key. The system must not allow masquerading or access by casual passers-by who may use an existing idle-state or paused machine.

Suitable password protection or encryption must be provided for company classified information on hard disk or other media that cannot be physically locked away.

Personal Computer Back-up and Recovery   Users of personal computers must be trained to establish and follow emergency recovery procedures, which might include periodic copying of critical files, including system software, to a floppy disk, followed by orderly and secure storage of such disks at a location different from that of the system.

Travel Security   Employees who carry personal computers while traveling should be trained to practice prudent security. Guidelines are as follows:

- Avoid using airline club or hotel-provided computers, which may have virus software and which could result in the loss of data to parties unknown.
- Protect all disks and tapes. Never leave company information media in a hotel room. Lock such materials in the hotel safe or carry them with you.
- Use caution when entering passwords in a public place.

- Use caution when working on a computer in an airplane, airport lounge, or hotel lobby. Assume people in the area are not friendly.
- Never place company information or media in checked baggage.

SUMMARY

Computer security requires attention to myriad details. The company should assign a skilled, experienced computer security manager.

NOTES

1. United States National Research Council, *Computers at Risk* (1991).
2. Morrie Gasser, *Building a Secure Computer System* (New York: Van Nostrand Reinhold, 1988), 3.
3. Steve Lipner, The Mitre Corporation, personal communication.

9

Communications Security

All business information at some point in its life cycle is in electronic form. In almost all cases information is transmitted over a network one or more times during use in business. Reports in the news about the information superhighway, the global village, and digital video services reflect the increasing use of electronic systems, networks, and media as the principal means of business communication.

Almost all communications are now digital-based and are processed through various computer hardware and software facilities. Even voice communication—not too long ago an example of a purely analog system—is now mostly digital. The private branch exchange (PBX), where the telephone operator once reigned, in most cases is now a microcomputer.

Most of the computer security measures discussed in chapter 8 apply to communications systems. There are sufficient differences in both risks and safeguards, however, to make further discussion worthwhile.

TYPES OF COMMUNICATIONS APPLICATIONS

Electronic data interchange (EDI), local area network (LAN), and wide area network (WAN) are illustrations of modern communications applications. These applications may be built on any of a number of configurations, including star networks and point-to-point networks, and delivery may be direct or through store-and-forward systems. In any case, the concern of the business manager is that information be communicated efficiently for the service requirements of the application and that the integrity and privacy of the message be maintained.

THE KEY QUESTIONS

For any communications system key security questions are the following:

- Who is sending and who is receiving the message?
- Is message integrity assured?
- Can delivery be proved?

If the responsible business manager can answer yes to these questions with certainty, security is satisfactory.

ASSURING COMMUNICATIONS SECURITY

As discussed later in this chapter, many security measures involve communications systems and networks. However, seeking resolutions to the three key questions invariably leads to the conclusion that security, reliability, and integrity must rely on the use of encryption, which is discussed later. Without encryption, there is simply no way to assure communications security.

COMMUNICATIONS RISKS

Communications system (network) vulnerabilities vary according to the transmission medium (wire, radio) and the distance serviced by the medium (WAN, LAN). In general, these risks can be identified as the following:

- *Eavesdropping*, in which an unauthorized person or program surreptitiously observes communications traffic and copies or otherwise collects the information contained in the traffic
- *Interception*, in which an unauthorized person or program retrieves a message and then secretly reinserts it into the network, perhaps having made changes to the message content
- *Masquerading*, in which an unauthorized person or program sends messages that appear to be genuine and that a recipient may believe to be from an authorized, authenticated sender

Case

An individual stole telephone company technical instruction manuals from waste containers. From those he was able to bypass telephone system computer controls and access engineering computers in a large company. By reading electronic mail at the company, the perpetrator was able to use employee account names and passwords and to masquerade as those employees. Eventually, he was successful in stealing valuable materials through clever manipulation of various systems and processes.

As the case shows, the risks may be combined. For example, an unauthorized person intercepts a message and then resends it, masquerading as another person (probably as the original authorized originator). Eavesdropping may involve wiretaps, interception of radio transmissions (usually satellite transmissions), collection of emanations, or observation of messages through carelessness on the part of the sender or the servicing communications provider. Interception may use a wiretap, so that the unauthorized observer of traffic can interrupt the flow of messages to allow replacement of traffic. Or, it may involve a radio antenna in the footprint of a broadcast. Masquerading can be done with wiretaps (direct connection to the physical circuit), by gaining access to one of the authorized entry points to a network, or by establishing an unauthorized entry point (for example, dial-up and password guessing).

NETWORK AND SERVICE VULNERABILITIES

Any voice or data network that carries clear-text traffic (data that are not encrypted) represents a severe information vulnerability. The following are reasons for this vulnerability:

- Companies cannot afford to buy long-line communications facilities. Simple economics dictates that services be purchased from utility companies licensed to provide such services. Once the data are on the public networks, the originator loses control over the information. The data may be transmitted on varying paths over different circuits involving wires or radio and may pass through several switching centers, where it can be observed by unauthorized persons or programs.
- It is difficult to ascertain with certainty exactly who is sending messages unless encryption is used.
- Messages may be misaddressed or misdirected through administrative errors by the originator or by mishandling en route. Consider electronic data interchange (EDI), the sending of business forms such as purchase orders over networks; mishandling is an invitation to fraud.
- Many networks operate as store-and-forward systems. That is, messages are collected and held, usually on disk, until the addressee asks to read mail. The information on the storage medium is subject to the usual risks of penetration, tampering, or unauthorized observation.
- Some network processes broadcast all traffic. For example, with Ethernet all messages are sent to all stations. The correct station, one hopes, retrieves only its own messages as the traffic goes by. An unauthorized station masquerading as an authorized station can collect all the messages intended for the genuine addressee.

Case

Security managers for a large multinational company were conducting a review of security measures at a large data center. They observed a service engineer from the telephone utility who was performing line quality checks. The security managers were dumbfounded when the unannounced and supposed highly confidential periodic financial results of the company's European division appeared in clear text on the service technician's screen.

INTEGRITY OF NETWORK TRAFFIC

A number of methods can be used to secure communications traffic integrity. These include CHECKSUM, parity checks, read-backs (ACK/NACK), and similar processes. Clever penetrations or interceptions may be able to defeat some of these measures. Effective network information security is obtained only through encryption.

CRYPTOGRAPHY OR ENCRYPTION

Cryptography is the science of transformation of characters to ensure secrecy or to prove identity. The implementation of the science in operational situations is called *encryption*. In its simplest form, cryptography is the substitution of one character for another. A simple substitution is called a Caesar cipher, for example *A = 1, B = 2*, and so forth. Modern cryptography provides complex, nonrepetitive substitutions. For example, *A = @, B = 2, C = P*, and so forth; in a subsequent occurrence in the same message, *A = M, B = X*, and *C = &*. The actual selection of the substituted characters is done with a mathematical algorithm. The algorithm processes the incoming clear text (human-readable text) against a key. This key is usually a large number or a word phrase. The key must be protected at the same level as the information being transmitted. In effect, one who has the key has the information.

Methods and Implementations

Two cryptographic methods are discussed briefly herein—*private key systems*, such as the widely used Data Encryption Standard (DES), and *public key systems*, such as the Rivest-Shamir-Adelman (RSA) method. For a more complete technical discussion, see Davies and Price's *Security for Computer Networks* (John Wiley & Sons, 1987).

Cryptographic services may be implemented through software programs or through computer hardware devices. The latter provide more economical, efficient processing, but software encryption systems offer greater utility for the occasional user.

Implementations of cryptography may be selective or general. In *selective* implementation, a company may provide services that allow users to encrypt messages assigned only certain company information classifications. Usually these would be only messages that have the highest, most sensitive classification. In *general* implementation, the company may choose to encrypt all traffic on certain circuits, having determined that most sensitive traffic follows those routes. The risk to sensitive traffic on other circuits may be considered acceptable because those messages are buried in hundreds or thousands of others that have little value.

In practice, a number of problems arise when encryption is applied to business circumstances. These include the following:

- Who is to have the key?
- How are those authorized to have the key to be provided with it (remember it must be kept secret)?
- Because any password or key must be assumed to have a decreasing work factor (it becomes more widely known or easier to compute) over time, the key must periodically be replaced. How is this to be done?

Managing Encryption Keys

Various methods are used to allow secure key management. Master keys (generated by computer random-number generating systems) may be loaded into hardware encryption devices directly by means of an encrypted message or with portable key-loading devices.

The master key is not known to any person. It is stored in one-way encrypted format and, in addition to being used to decipher encrypted messages, can be used to identify each node or station on a network.

A *session* is a period of time during which messages are transmitted. *Session keys* may be changed automatically by the system each time a new data stream or assembly of data packets is sent. The session key has the advantage of presenting a new challenge periodically to anyone who may be working at discovery of keys.

When cryptographic service is initiated, a key may be delivered to the authorized user physically by means of registered mail or courier. Or, it may be entered without exposure to humans into an encryption device with a key generator mechanism, which is delivered and used by a trusted person.

Key changes are handled by means of encryption of the new key with the old key and sending it over the network. Of course, if the old key has been compromised, the new one may be immediately exposed. A better process involves a *master key*. Master keys are used to identify authorized recipients of new session keys. The master key is used to encrypt the new session key for each node. A key-management system in the central security computer keeps track of key changes.

Cryptographic key distribution and management is one of the most important causes of the large overhead that has plagued the use of any cryptographic technique. The problem is that cryptographic keys (typically 64-bit random numbers) have to be shared with absolute secrecy between the creator and the user of the data. If the key is known to anyone else, security is compromised. The problem is compounded by the fact that there may be several keys for each creator-user pair.

Security hardware separates key management from business computer applications, allowing the programmer to concentrate on the application itself. Modern encryption key management systems provide facilities for defining, creating, exchanging, storing, and destroying cryptographic keys. Both point-to-point and key distribution center modes of operation are supported.

Public Key Systems

The public key encryption method is based on characteristics of very large prime numbers. It is computationally infeasible to solve for the factors of the product of two large prime numbers. Therefore, it is possible to encrypt a message with a private key known only to the sender. However, the person encrypting the message and the addressee of the message each have a public key, which might be published in a directory. The message is further encrypted with the addressee's public key. On receipt, the addressee decrypts the message with the sender's public key and then further decrypts using his or her own private key. This arrangement not only assures privacy and integrity for the message but also proves that the sender is the one who owns that public key used. Otherwise, the message would not change to clear text when decrypted.

Key management and other critical matters, such as positive sender authentication, may be resolved with the public key process. Public key systems are attractive because they provide the highest level of security and also because they have been standardized in the American National Standards Institute ANSI X9.n series and in the International Organization for Standardization (ISO) equivalent standards.

Modern encryption hardware systems dramatically reduce the cost of using cryptographic techniques by providing simple, standard, programming interfaces and management facilities. Specialized expertise is no longer needed; cryptographic protection is available to all applications at a much reduced cost. For example, Digital Equipment Corporation offers products that provide the following range of services:

- Message authentication (ANSI X9.9)
- Cryptographic key distribution and management (ANSI X9.17)
- Application-level encryption
- Encryption hardware support
- Management facilities, including security audit trails

Message Authentication Codes

Message authentication codes (MACs) are used to ensure that there has been no unauthorized modification of information. A MAC is a cryptographic CHECKSUM added to data before they are stored or transmitted across a network. When the data are accessed, the MAC is checked by recalculation and comparison with the original value. It is impossible to make an unauthorized change to the data and a corresponding change to the MAC. Thus the integrity of the data can be guaranteed. A typical use of a MAC is in electronic funds transfer (EFT). A MAC ensures that the transfer amount or the account data have not been altered en route.

TELEPHONE SYSTEM SECURITY

PBX systems are now microcomputers. These systems can be attacked by so-called hackers, who can gain control and cause much misery and mischief.

Case

A company installed a telephone PBX microcomputer from a large supplier. Later, telephone charges for long distance calls were investigated and found to amount to tens of thousands of dollars. Most of the calls were unauthorized. Subsequent investigation showed that all the microcomputers provided by that supplier were delivered with the same three-digit password control. Clever hackers could merely dial in and gain sufficient control to make unlimited long distance calls.

Business managers must not regard telephone systems and facilities as unimportant. Traditional business practices such as storing cleaning supplies in the communications closet are simply unacceptable today. Telephone computers require careful security management. Access to telephone computers and knowledge of the passwords should be based on strict business needs. Telephone wiring and system spaces should be kept locked at all times.

Radio Telephones

A corollary matter is the use of portable or radio (car) telephones. These instruments broadcast in the FM ranges, and transmissions are readily intercepted by simple scanners available at radio supply stores or even by use of UHF television receivers.

Case

A company made a large portion of its profits from servicing machinery. It was discovered that service business was being lost to a small competitor. Investigation showed that service call dispatch orders, communicated by car phone, were being intercepted. The competitor was able to arrive on the scene first, and in some cases got the business.

SPECIAL CONSIDERATIONS

Electronic data interchange (EDI) is transmission of documents or forms in digital form. For example, a purchase order is sent to a supplier electronically by means of a form created in a computer application. No paper exists. The risks include interception, claims of nonreceipt, misaddressing, loss of accountability, and unauthorized modification of data. EDI systems must be carefully designed to establish financial controls, to provide proofs of integrity, and to allow proof of receipt. Encryption would seem to be a solution, although it is seldom used for EDI.

A *local area network (LAN)* is a building or campus network operated as a unit and connected to an external telecommunications system through a gateway device. LAN systems are notorious for poor security, especially if network-connected devices are available to a community of people who can connect without positive identification. Some LAN systems allow almost casual attachment of additional devices, and the use of a clandestine terminal masquerading as another authorized node is not unusual. Devices and wires used in any LAN deserve special security attention. Unfortunately, in many cases even rudimentary physical security is lacking. Positive user identification to establish responsibility for actions should be provided through proper passwords or other authentication methods.

SUMMARY

Networks are an integral part of business operations. Information of all kinds travels over internal and public networks by wire and radio, and much of this information is proprietary and thus requires protection. Businesses should consider encryption as a routine practice to safeguard information, which, although normally protected inside company facilities, may be at risk in radio or wire transmission.

Part III

Information Security Management

Information Security
Management

10

Information Security in the Business Enterprise

I don't get involved with information. I stick to the investigations and property protection.

Security director of a large United States company

Security is a widely accepted but little understood business function. Remarkably, over a period of more than one hundred years, business management has seemingly failed to bring security "into the business." As a result, security is often viewed as a necessary evil, a burden from which there is no relief because of human failings, threats, and vulnerabilities related to societal problems.

In some cases the security function does not relate to the business because security managers are often military or police people who have a mentality far removed from that of the entrepreneurial manager, who may relish a risk taken and a reward won. Security people tend to think in terms of absolutes. That is, they have a book solution for every risk, and no alternative is recognized or offered.

In other cases security is kept separate from business because business leaders do not want to be involved with what they consider the "seamy" side of conducting business. They want to think of their employees as loyal and honest. Proof to the contrary is unpleasant and disquieting.

Security managers recognize their status with comments such as, "If nothing goes wrong, the boss says, 'What do I need you for?' If something does happen, he says, 'Where were you when this happened?' "

Security is becoming ever more necessary and ever more expensive, and business management should pull security into the business operation. Senior management should insist that security be managed like any other operational activity, with plans and demonstrated results. It is difficult to prove the results of many asset-protection activities, but probably no more so than to prove the results of an investment in advertising or charity. Many business investments are necessary and have a return that cannot be measured in hard, demonstrable statistics.

The easy case is with investigations and recoveries. For most medium-sized to large companies, the value of recoveries (property or product recovered, frauds or defamations stopped) easily justifies an investment in investigative resources. For information security, however, justifying the relatively large investment needed is not simple. The apparent absence of loss of information may be considered to demonstrate that little or no threat exists. However, the appearance that information is not being lost may only be an indication that information is not controlled. Unfortunately when an attack on information succeeds, the results often have serious effects on profitability, costs, or reputation.

Business justification for information security has two bases. These are as follows:

1. The value or sensitivity assigned to the various information elements used in the business, usually referred to as *information classification*
2. The risks perceived through knowledge and awareness of the company's information vulnerabilities and societal threats

An example is a company that has many computers connected to networks but has never been aware of problems with so-called hackers. A cursory reading of the business press quickly leads a business manager to an objective conclusion that there is a serious risk that, without security, the company's computers may be taken over by computer hackers. If astute, the manager decides that security is an insurance policy needed to protect the business.

Case

During a visit from the inspector general, a senior information system manager at a military support organization was asked for the emergency recovery plan. His reply was that "we don't have an emergency plan because we have never had a disaster."

Of course, a business that has had bitter experience with hackers or with an embarrassing or damaging theft of information already has motivation for security. But even in such a case, it is difficult to justify security investment in the usual terms of return on investment.

Case

Engineers in an electronics firm had refused to apply security measures to their computers. After repeated attacks by outside computer hackers that required constant rebuilding of complex software, company management directed that a program be undertaken to strengthen security, and the engineers were forced to comply.

THE BASIS FOR INVESTMENT IN INFORMATION SECURITY

Much of the information used in a business does not warrant protection. The process of determining which information needs to be protected is called *information classification*. Classification relates to value or sensitivity.

Classification is the first and primary base for justifying information security investment.

It is postulated that in most businesses about 30 percent of information justifies an investment in the various means for protection. The business may consider that the remaining 70 percent is private to the company but probably not worth the effort necessary to provide real protection. Assuming that the company has identified three levels of classification, it can be estimated on the basis of practice at many successful businesses that about 1 percent of information falls into the top, most restrictive classification. About 10 percent of information falls into each of the other two categories.

A secondary base for determining the appropriate spending level for information protection is information-related risk.

Information-related risk is determined by management and refers to the following:

1. The potential for information security failures or vulnerability.
2. The possible damage if information is exposed, improperly changed, destroyed, or denied.

The decision on risk must be related to management's stated risk acceptance posture. That is, how much information risk is the business willing to accept?

Chapter 5 describes the technical process of information classification. It is worth noting here that information vulnerabilities include physical, electronic, and mental threats that may result in loss of information privacy, integrity, reliability, or proprietary rights. Information protection, then, involves a number of functional specialists, including legal counsel, computer system specialists, personnel experts, and security people.

Information classification is a shared responsibility. Although the security manager is primarily responsible for information protection, the decision about classification almost always rests with the senior manager responsible for the business activity originating or budgeting for the information in question. Usually this responsibility is connected to data management functions. The responsible manager may be called the information custodian, data owner, or a similar title.

In some cases highly sensitive information may have only a brief useful life and therefore not require protection. Other information may not be highly sensitive but needs to be kept confidential over a long period of time, and so needs strong protection. In other instances, information that costs little may have great competitive value. Retention schedules for information, typically for documents and electronic files, should be established by company record-management plans, which must include the provision of proper security according to the established company classification.

Classification, if it is to serve its purpose, is based on intimate knowledge of the business and how and why the particular piece of information is used and valued. This knowledge is seldom available to the security manager and staff. It must come from the business managers.

THE PROPER MANAGEMENT VIEW

If security is to be effective, and if the business is to realize a prudent return on its investment in security, security must be seen as and made to be an essential, working part of the business enterprise.

Good organization includes consistent assignment of responsibilities. The business security manager should be responsible for protecting all assets of a company. The most important assets include people, information, materials, products, and facilities. Security is both an art and a science. Professional security managers should be hired because they have the experience and technical skills needed to provide good security for all of the company's assets.

The company security director or manager should be knowledgeable in the various technologies involved. These include computing, closed-circuit television, electronic physical access-control systems, and security software applications. This does not mean the security manager must be able to write computer software or maintain operating system security. It does mean that he or she must be familiar with the methods and purposes of such activity.

There is a historic tendency to assign information security to other than the security department, and this is an error. Companies do not assign the protection of manufacturing plants to the manufacturing manager, although he or she certainly knows more about manufacturing than does the security manager. No special technical skill is needed to develop and implement information security in the broad corporate sense, which is what management should want the security manager to do.

COMPONENTS OF THE BUSINESS SECURITY FUNCTION

To understand how information security fits into a business security plan, one must understand the overall function of security. The kinds of security activities in the typical business enterprise include controls over property (machinery, vehicles, office equipment), information, and materials; control of access to company facilities; provision of physical security measures necessary to safeguard company employees; electronic measures; and surveillance of company real estate. These are generic security activities, seen from the functional security viewpoint. Information security work falls into several of these security categories.

Employee and Personal Protection   Employee and personal protection includes security for people at work, management of crises (e.g., kidnapping of an employee), protection for special events, protection for employees who travel or live in foreign countries, and general security awareness and training.

Employee Quality   Employee quality involves reference checking for new employees, substance abuse programs, governmental security clearance management, and training appropriate to these matters.

Procedures   Procedures include instructions for the control of company property, information, and materials, usually in the form of policies and standards (e.g., information protection procedures); procedures for use by employees in the course of their work; audits; and security reviews.

Investigations   Investigations involve suspected violations of company policies or violations of law on company premises. These investigations may be conducted in secret (undercover) if circumstances warrant.

Electronic Protection   Electronic protection includes closed-circuit television monitoring, proximity detection, and technical countermeasures (e.g., a sweep of a room to determine if listening devices are present); logical information security measures implemented through computer hardware and software (e.g., identification, authentication, and authorization of computer users); and network security software.

THE BUSINESS ENTERPRISE VIEW

An executive or high-level view of the security function and the place and content of information security is shown in Figure 10–1.

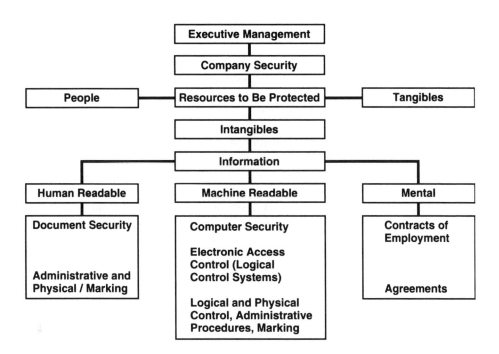

Figure 10–1   The enterprise view of security.

In a business enterprise, a properly constituted security function has responsibility for protection of all company resources and assets. These assets can be identified as people, information, financial wealth, land and facilities, equipment, and raw materials.

There are three broad management goals for information security, which are discussed in chapters 5 and 6:

1. To identify the most critical and valuable elements of information through proper information classification in order to direct limited security investments to the most important efforts and to allow management's risk acceptance decisions to be implemented
2. To protect company information in all forms, and as appropriate according to the classification, from unauthorized transfer, observation, modification, or destruction
3. To establish the company's claims of proprietary rights to information that may have important competitive or market implications. Such action may become necessary if the protections fail and such a claim in a court of law be necessary or appropriate.

Within the company's security plan, information security represents a broad area of responsibility. It includes the provision of business-related processes for the following:

*   Evaluation (classification) of information
*   Granting authority to access and modify information
*   Marking, handling, transfer, mailing or transmission, storage, and destruction of information

These responsibilities apply to information in all three general forms–mental, written (paper, microforms, pictures, transparencies), and electronic (in computer process, in storage in core or memory, on disks, cartridges, or tapes, and in transmission over networks).

Information security is a large part of enterprise security, along with the protection of physical assets and people. Electronic information security, paper information security, and mental information security are components of information security. Within electronic information security is computer security, which includes network security.

Understanding of the business security structure, or an equivalent structure suited to a particular situation, is a prerequisite for construction of an effective, practical information security process. Providing security in bits and pieces (e.g., securing the computers) can only result in a waste of effort and disappointing results.

VIEWPOINTS

Information security can mean different things to various organizations and people depending on their business, experience, organizational placement, training, and environment. Examples are as follows:

- Readers of the popular press and watchers of television news may believe that information security consists of warding off brilliant teen-age computer hackers.
- Computer operators and users of personal computers may see information security as the proper use of passwords, account authorizations, and protection of data centers.
- Readers of business magazines and newspapers may think of information security as consisting of protections against industrial espionage.
- Secretaries might consider sealing envelopes and stamping documents information security.
- Managers may consider information security to be merely something the secretary should know about and worry about.

Each of these views may be partially correct and therefore is dangerous. If a security program works only in one dimension, it fails in its primary task.

Effective information protection results when information in any form is properly assigned a company information classification to indicate its value and need for protection and when suitable protection is provided as appropriate to that assigned classification. Management cannot afford to be swayed by press hyperbole or technical fascination. Information protection must be a careful and deliberate process.

Case

A senior executive met the company security manager in the company cafeteria queue and asked, "How's computer security?" The security manager replied, "That's the wrong question. You should have asked, 'How's information security?' "

Once a decision has been made to protect information, the organization must be correctly aligned with other security responsibilities. The process must include all information forms in a consistent manner. There is no point to providing strong locks on the front door if the back door is to be left open.

ORGANIZATION

Responsibility for information security must be correctly placed if the investment in security is to have the desired results. Too often responsibility for information protection is assigned on a casual or ad hoc basis, giving a clear message that the subject is really not an important one. Figure 10–2 illustrates a correct business organization for information protection. Certainly there are others ways to organize that could be equally effective. The following two cogent points must be made:

1. The information security officer should not report to an administrator who has primary responsibility for information (Figure 10–3).

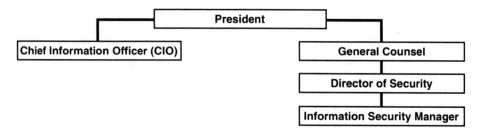

Figure 10–2   Correct organizational placement of information security function.

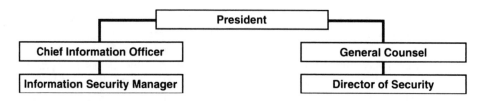

Figure 10–3   Incorrect placement reflecting confusion of computer security with information security.

2. Information security must be placed so that problems are addressed, not covered up. Information security should be a function of the company security department. In turn, the security director should report to corporate audit, corporate legal counsel, or a similar high-level officer with extensive oversight responsibilities (Figure 10–2).

SUMMARY

Correct understanding of the overall security responsibility is a prerequisite to establishment of effective information security.

11

Relating Information Security Investment to Business Needs

Correct strategic diagnosis is an absolute prerequisite for successful use of computers. A misdirection in goals can doom a project before it begins. A diagnosis that pinpoints what needs fixing can tolerate unimpressive technical solutions. Picking the wrong priorities will nullify whatever sophisticated technologies and excellent people could produce.

Paul A. Strassmann, *The Business Value of Computers* (New Canaan, Conn.: Information Economics Press, 1990), 183.

The purpose of business in a capitalist system is profit. Any cost that does not contribute to activity resulting in profit is overhead expense. Managers of companies usually want to control and, if possible, eliminate overhead expense. Here we have the makings of the dilemma faced by security managers: How can we relate security spending requests to the business of making a profit? This chapter addresses that issue.

THROUGH THE BUSINESS MANAGER'S EYES

Most business managers do not see information security as an important business issue. For the chief executive, information security—or even security per se—is probably not on the list of top one hundred issues. The company's chief information officer (CIO) may be more aware of information security, but it is probably not a matter of keen interest unless a recent breach of information security is fresh in mind.

This discussion begins with the problem that what security managers believe to be of paramount importance may not be seen by their superiors—those who must approve budget requests—to be critical to the business.

The views of most business managers are as follows:

- Security is a matter that should be kept out of sight and out of mind. Let others handle it.
- Warnings and gloomy predictions are not welcomed. They do not sit well in the councils of those who are risk-takers by nature.

- Information is intangible. Managers find it difficult to conceptualize the risks involved until a serious incident occurs.
- Much of the information protection methodology is complex and deals with legal and technical matters. Busy managers resent having to take time to understand these issues. Usually, they do not.
- Computers are involved with many information security problems. Most business managers—even those who may use a personal computer or workstation—are seldom familiar with the technical aspects of computer use. Explanations purporting to justify investments in logical security may simply not be understood.
- The risks and vulnerabilities associated with information are difficult to identify or to quantify. Consequently, it is not easy to assign values or to project probabilities of occurrence. Managers are unlikely to be enthusiastic about investment proposals based on a guess multiplied by an estimate.
- The business effects of actual information losses or exposures may not be readily quantified. Even after a business secret is exposed or a business file improperly changed, it is often difficult to prove the effects on business.
- Employees outside the security function probably do not see security as their responsibility. Yet security is real only if everyone participates to the appropriate degree.
- Reports of breaches of information security are not plausible to most managers. At one time a figure of $500,000 was reported as the average loss due to computer-related crime. This figure was considered high by most business managers. However, because most managements keep losses and problems secret and because they usually choose not to go to court, there are not good data to back up projections of risk.

Case

A computer hacker broke into a company's network and was able to obtain a copy of an extremely valuable piece of software. However, during investigation of the incident, the software was recovered. The thief seemed not to recognize what he had acquired. The company could not demonstrate a business effect; it could only provide conjectures about a loss.

Case

A private memo intended for only a few senior executives was leaked to a newspaper. The memo created a stir among employees and investors. It was difficult to assess the real business impact, although the embarrassment was real.

To succeed in their work, security managers must find ways to relate information security more closely to the business process.

THE DECISION TO BEGIN

In most cases, company management decides to become serious about information security after an incident concerning information exposure, loss, or litigation imposes costs on the business. In other instances the board of directors or senior management may have read a report or heard a story about liability arising from careless information handling. Or perhaps the CIO has made a recommendation that information security is needed.

Once senior management has decided to proceed with a program of information security, a method is required to make this effort relate to business needs in terms of what is done and how much it costs. Security is always a business decision.

Information security must follow from business decisions made by those responsible for the content of the information. Security managers should be the protection experts and should provide advice on vulnerabilities and security measures.

RESPONSIBILITIES

In most companies, responsibility for the content of information (not the same as custody of information, which may be the purview of information systems or information management) is diffused throughout the organization. That is, the various elements of information are originated by and their content is established by various functional managers. These managers are called *data owners*. Accounting information is the responsibility of the accounting manager, personnel information is the responsibility of the personnel manager, work-in-process information is the responsibility of the manufacturing manager, and so forth.

Some sets of information may be generated by a number of different activities and then consolidated into one file or database. In today's information environment, in which distributed systems may be connected with large databases, the identity of the functional data owner may not be clear. In such a case, the data probably belong to the manager who budgets for the system application development or who pays the largest share for operation of the application. Information ownership may have to be decided by senior management. Just as "someone" must assume responsibility for approving application modifications, so must someone accept responsibility for information ownership. These data owners have the best overview or insight into appropriate information classification decisions. They best know about the value or sensitivity of any given element of information within their area of responsibility. Value or sensitivity is the basis for assigning information classifications, and classification is the basis for determination of appropriate investment in information protection measures.

Classification usually points to a menu of security measures established by the security function. For example, assignment of the highest (most sensitive or valuable) classification to a particular element of information indicates that encryption should be used when such information is transmitted on a network. Classification is a decision by the data owner or functional manager responsible. The menu of security measures related to classification is provided by security experts.

A company's security standards (see chapter 12) should specify this classification–security measures menu relationship. Because information responsibility (data ownership) is diffuse, the business should establish a representative committee or group to develop and pursue appropriate information security strategies. This group should probably include corporate security, information systems or information management, administration, office services, network management, and the various functional or organizational groups. It is impossible to specify the best, appropriate membership without intimate knowledge of the organization and work of a particular business. However, the group should be one that assures representation of all important information security–related interests and sufficient coverage and weight (political, organizational) to allow the committee to make effective decisions on behalf of the members' constituencies across the company. If the committee must have various managements validate every decision, the make-up of the committee is probably not correct.

For convenience in this book the committee is called the Information Security Committee (ISC). At a minimum the ISC implements an information security program, which would set information protection policy that meets management's established risk acceptance goals. The policy, which establishes the information classification process, leads to information protection standards. These standards establish the company-wide procedures and methods that provide security in a manner and at a price consistent with business constraints.

Table 11–1 illustrates the basic information security management process.

THE THREE-DIMENSIONAL PROCESS

A common problem in establishing and maintaining an information security program is completeness. For example, who has the responsibility for the many decisions and tasks involved? What are the component issues and tasks necessary?

A process for managing information security, one involving a fairly collegiate committee, is suggested. The overall goals are to connect the information security effort to the complex, dynamic requirements of modern business. To be effective, the process should gain commitment throughout the company for information security investments. This process is called the *Defensive Set Three-dimensional Matrix*.

Table 11–1   Basic Information Security Management Process

1. Management decides to establish information security program (M)
2. Management and security write policy regarding definitions for information protection and classification (Defensive Set process) (M, S)
3. Security experts define security measures and relate these to the classifications defined (Defensive Set process) (S)
4. Functional information owners assign classifications (ongoing process: there are both permanent classifications and ad hoc classifications) (F)
5. Information security strategies provide impetus for development and maintenance of the program (Defensive Set process) (ISC)
6. Security standards relate classifications to the security measures menu and provide implementing instructions for all forms of information—written, electronic, mental (Defensive Set process) (ISC)
7. Auditors evaluate program effectiveness (A)

KEY: A = auditors, F = functional information owners, ISC = information security committee, M = senior management, S = security managers.

The three-dimensional process establishes the relationships among ongoing business operational requirements and the necessary investments in information security policies, commitment, and strategies. The three-dimensional process uses terms and concepts from football as a basis for making wise information security management decisions.

The Three-dimensional Defensive Set

The Defensive Set provides a three-dimensional view of the "field" of information security in a large organization and provides for management and strategy development in an organized, structured manner (Figure 11–1).

Defensive Set 3D Matrix

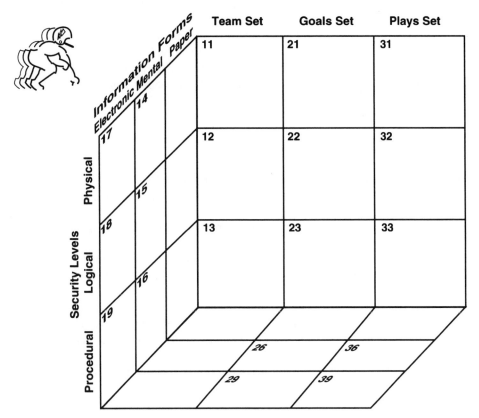

Note: Cubes numbered 24, 25, 27, 28, 34, 35, 37, and 38 are hidden in this view.

Figure 11–1   The Defensive Set three-dimensional matrix. Copyright 1995, James A. Schweitzer. All rights reserved.

The Defensive Set matrix is a self-study of information security, including in one plane its component team sets, goals, and plays, conceptualized in three-dimensional form. A second plane identifies the forms of information, and the third plane allows specification of commitment, policy, and strategy. The activity of identifying and listing all these elements is an important learning process for information managers and others properly involved, such as auditors and administrators.

The Defensive Set provides a list of the organizational, procedural, and technical security elements involved in information security. It also provides a general plan of action in the *plays set*.

The Three-dimensional View

The Defensive Set provides a multidimensional view of information security as it relates to business operations. The Defensive Set process provides an iterative consideration of requirements definition, strategy, implementation, measurement, and refinement. This process is continuous and should yield an always fresh business security plan as a basis for the company's strategic vision for information security. Only policy remains fairly static. Information security standards (see chapter 12) change as business changes.

The three-dimensional matrix provides a working tool for planning of and commitment to information security goals.

Applying the Three-dimensional Matrix

In the three-dimensional matrix there are twenty-seven cubes. Each cube represents the intersection of relationships among the nine aspects of information security, as follows:

- The front plane represents the *team set* (commitment of participants), the *goals set* (policy), and the *plays set* (standards).
- The side plane represents the information forms: *mental, paper,* and *electronic.*
- The end plane represents the levels of protection: *physical, logical,* and *procedural.*

Each intersection, or cube, provides an opportunity for an analysis leading to identification of the required participants, their commitments, and the necessary security actions. Attempting to perform this analysis without a structure is tedious and can easily omit necessary requirements.

Some cubes are *null* because protection does not apply. For example, there is no logical protection for mental information.

The Three-dimensional Process

Figures 11–2 through 11–28 illustrate the process of completing the three-dimensional Defensive Set analysis.

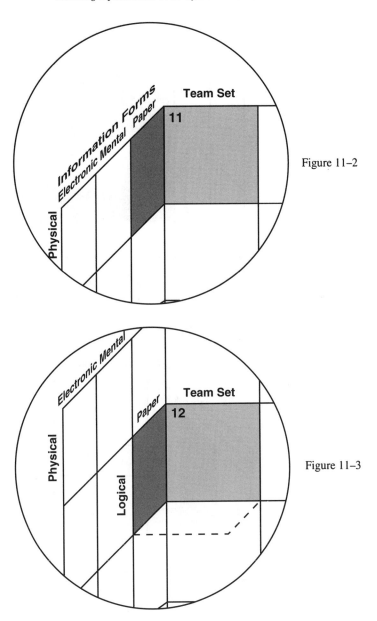

Figure 11–2

Figure 11–3

The team set for Cube 11 (Figure 11–2) is to identify and gain commitment from the organizational staffs essential to protection of information on paper, film, photographs, or other human-readable media. At minimum, the team should include the following functions, as established by policy: security, legal, personnel, administration. Physical protection includes (usually established by standards) document handling and storage and long-term records processing. Cube 12 (Figure 11–3) is a null cube. Logical elements are not appropriate for paper forms.

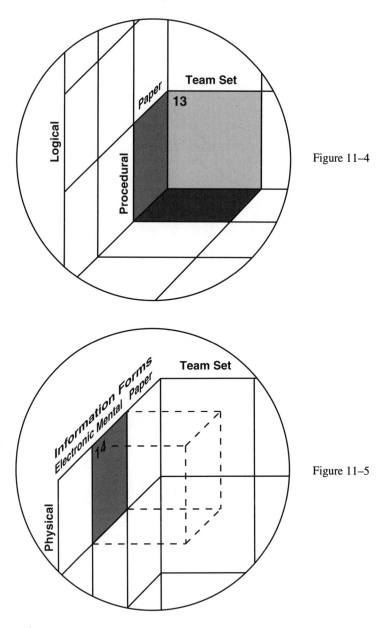

Figure 11–4

Figure 11–5

The team set for Cube 13 (Figure 11–4) includes security, administration, personnel, and legal departments. Procedures include classification by originator or information owner, classification marking, handling procedure, and end-of-life processes. Cube 14 (Figure 11–5) is a null cube. Physical protection is not appropriate for information in mental form.

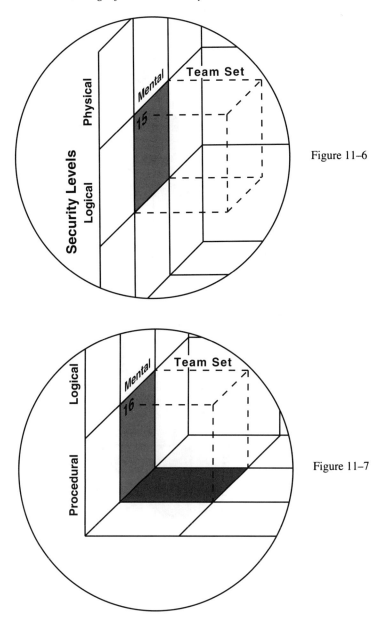

Figure 11–6

Figure 11–7

Cube 15 (Figure 11–6) is a null cube. Logical protection is not appropriate for information in mental form. The team set for Cube 16 (Figure 11–7) includes security, administration, and legal counsel. Procedures must provide for information disclosure agreements by all employees and by customers and contractors who have access to company classified information.

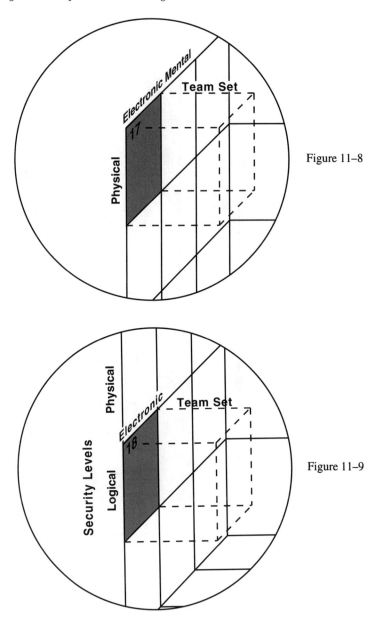

Figure 11–8

Figure 11–9

The team set for Cube 17 (Figure 11–8) includes security, information systems, and telecommunications. Physical protection includes restricted access to all operational sites, physical access controls and records, protection of media, and similar functions.

The team set for Cube 18 (Figure 11–9) includes security, system software staff, application development staff, and telecommunications staff. Logical elements include access-control software, system monitoring, and logging software.

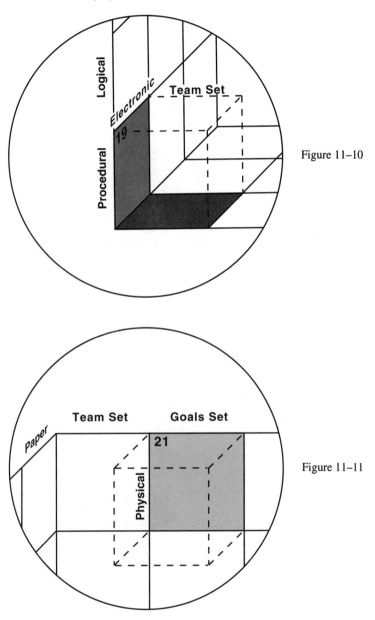

Figure 11–10

Figure 11–11

The team set for Cube 19 (Figure 11–10) includes security, information systems, and personnel. Procedures include access and privilege granting and control processes.

The goals set (policy) for Cube 21 (Figure 11–11) is as follows: protect all information forms as appropriate to classification; prevent casual or accidental unauthorized disclosure; handle and store information securely; and destroy information at end-of-life.

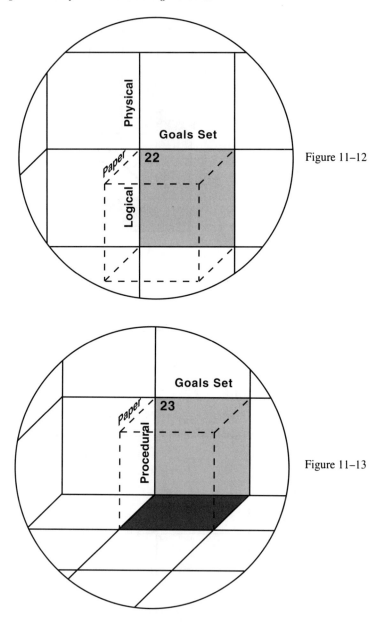

Figure 11–12

Figure 11–13

Cube 22 (Figure 11–12) is a null cube. Logical security is not used for protecting human-readable forms of information. The goals set (policy) for Cube 23 (Figure 11–13) is as follows: provide clear instructions for classification decisions; assure prompt classification at creation of new information; assure prompt, evident classification marking; provide for secure handling and storage; provide end-of-life process; and limit disclosure as appropriate to the assigned company class.

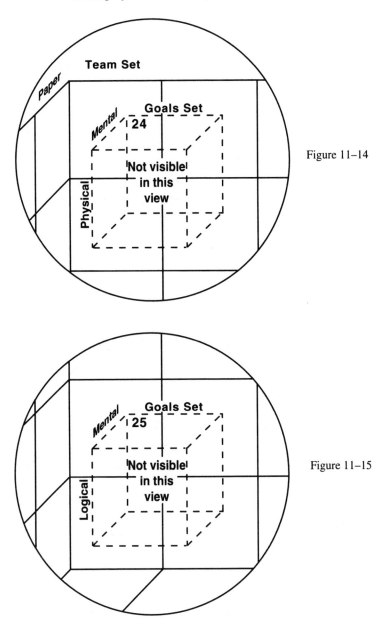

Figure 11–14

Figure 11–15

Cube 24 (Figure 11–14) is a null cube. Physical protection is not appropriate for the mental form of information.

Cube 25 (Figure 11–15) is a null cube. Logical security measures are not appropriate for mental information.

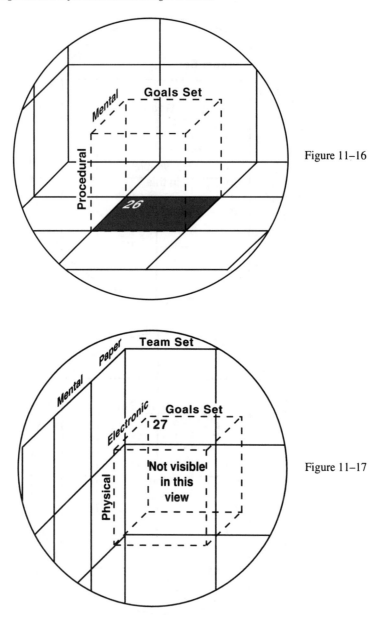

Figure 11–16

Figure 11–17

The procedural element goals (policy) for Cube 26 (Figure 11–16) are as follows: establish clear claims to information; define responsibilities of the various parties involved (managers, employees, suppliers, customers, procurement officers); and provide proper legal forms.

The goals set (policy) for Cube 27 (Figure 11–17) is as follows: protect all system and communications components and facilities; limit physical access to components and facilities; and provide redundancy and emergency back-up.

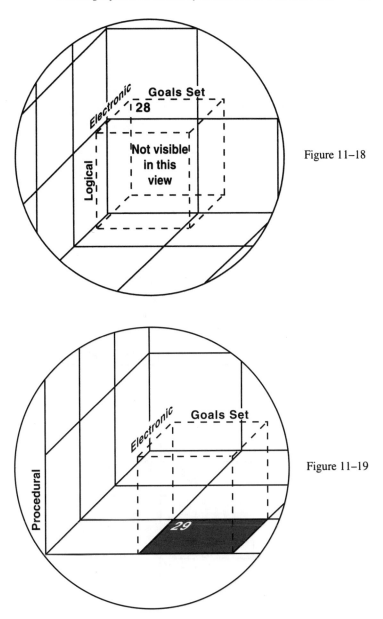

Figure 11–18

Figure 11–19

The goals set (policy) for Cube 28 (Figure 11–18) is as follows: identify all accessors and authenticate to allow authorized privileges only; limit access as a general rule; and monitor and react to suspected violations.

The goals set (policy) for Cube 29 (Figure 11–19) is as follows: authorize each user to least-privilege level required by job assessment; audit authorizations periodically; and control authorizations through effective management processes.

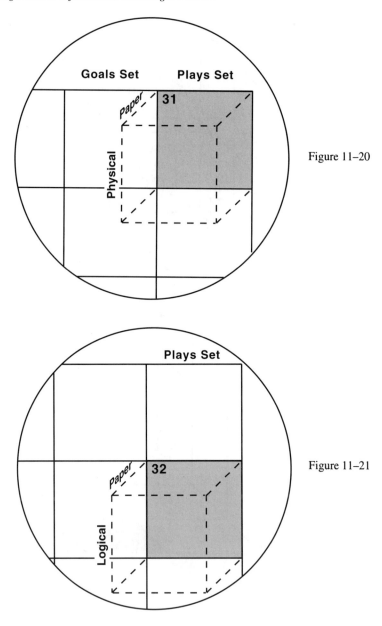

Figure 11–20

Figure 11–21

The plays set for Cube 31 (Figure 11–20) is as follows: set standards for secure storage (furniture, safes); establish access control for facilities; establish copier and facsimile controls; and others as required.

Cube 32 (Figure 11–21) is a null cube. Logical protection is not appropriate for human-readable forms of information.

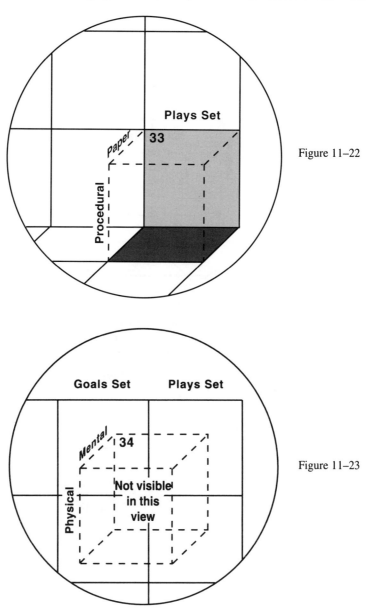

Figure 11–22

Figure 11–23

The plays set for Cube 33 (Figure 11–22) is to describe strategies to arrive at a goals set. These might include publishing policy and development of standards, including rules for assigning classification, marking, and handling at each classification level.

Cube 34 (Figure 11–23) is a null cube. Physical protection does not apply to mental forms of information.

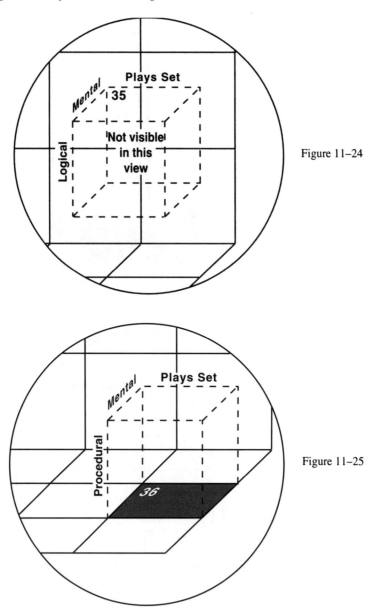

Figure 11–24

Figure 11–25

Cube 35 (Figure 11–24) is a null cube. Logical protection does not apply to mental forms of information.

The plays set for Cube 36 (Figure 11–25) is to establish the following legal procedures for protecting mental information: employment contracts to include disclosure agreements; disclosure agreements with consultants, contractors, suppliers, and customers; and periodic refreshment of such agreements.

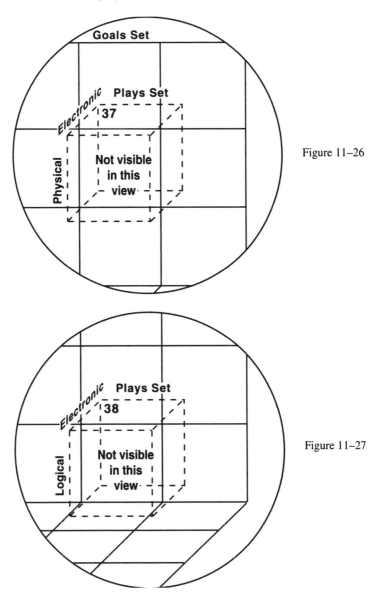

Figure 11–26

Figure 11–27

The plays set for Cube 37 (Figure 11–26) is to develop the standards (and procedures if needed) for the following: physical access controls for all data-processing and telecommunications facilities; limiting access to devices in any location as appropriate; and safeguarding all media.

The plays set for Cube 38 (Figure 11–27) is as follows: provide for identification and authentication of all users; provide encryption for high-value data; provide automatic surveillance and alarm software; provide classification-marking graphics; and limit access and delivery to authorized entities.

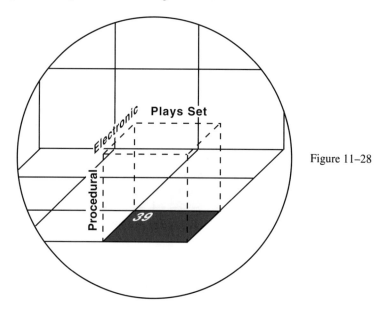

Figure 11–28

The plays set for Cube 39 (Figure 11–28) is as follows: set process for authorizing users; maintain auditable records; set controls for software updates; and other.

The Defensive Set process provides a foundation for development and management of a program for information security in the following ways:

- The process of completing the Defensive Set matrix clarifies understanding of the parts and complexities of information security.
- The Defensive Set process ensures that managers do not forget or overlook "players" or "plays" important to success.
- Development of entries for the matrix helps clarify where the real problems are. Managers, because of their involvement in day-to-day operation, often do not see the problems. The Defensive Set matrix forces a focus on issues.
- The matrix approach facilitates identification of and agreement on goals and increases common understanding about what needs to be done (plays) to succeed.
- The Defensive Set process provides a set of general rules against which to test decisions and policies. Business directives that look good in concept may prove to be seriously flawed once in operation. The matrix helps avoid "do overs."
- The cooperative nature of the Defensive Set process supports explanations to other departments and organizations and aids in obtaining their team's commitment to mutually supportive information security roles. The process helps clarify the role of audit, personnel, security force (guards) managers, risk managers, and financial controllers in the information security effort.
- The Defensive Set matrix helps drive the development of strategies (plays set), without which justification of investment, and progress, is difficult.

Results of the Defensive Set Process

In actual use, each cube provides a learning experience and produces the following benefits:

- Lists of necessary participants and their required commitments
- Descriptions of protection requirements to be established through publication of information security standards
- Technical measures appropriate to the cube, which may include purchase of software
- Knowledge about the complex function of information security
- Strategies that increase confidence as the fit between the security matrix and the business becomes obvious
- A resource, the matrix, that can be referred to when difficult decisions are made, allowing a validation of thought processes and conclusions against an established set of rules
- A tool, the matrix, that can be used as evidence to show management that information security is a business process and that it relates to business needs

Advantages to Using the Three-dimensional Matrix

The three-dimensional process is a tool for those selected to participate in defining the information security effort. Among the important advantages are the following:

- The team may find previously hidden resources.
- Participants needed are identified and made aware of their responsibilities.
- A complete picture of the information security environment is developed, helping assure a complete security effort.

INFORMATION SECURITY STRATEGY

The goals developed with the Defensive Set matrix form the background for sound strategy decisions. Each business must develop goals appropriate to its unique circumstances and to the relative value and sensitivity of information to the business. However, some general goals are as follows:

1. Provide appropriate information security, across all functions, and for all information forms (paper, electronic, mental).
2. Establish an integrated set of cross-functional corporate policies (permanent) and corporate-organizational information security standards (change to meet dynamic business operational circumstances).
3. Encourage personal acceptance of individual employee responsibility for information security by setting simple, practical security requirements.
4. Establish and coordinate simple, business-related procedures for worldwide information security incident management and reporting.

5. Provide information security knowledge through the development and use of innovative, effective educational materials and through development of management support for the information security effort.

The Defensive Set identifies the responsibilities of the various company organizations with regard to information security issues and coordinated response to security issues.

INFORMATION PROTECTION RESPONSIBILITIES

Descriptions of responsibilities should include functions, employee groups, committees, and individual employees who must protect business information. The matrix defines information security interrelationships and responsibilities. Typical definitions include the following.

Corporate Security Officer   Corporate security is the organization responsible for the overall leadership of the company security function, including all aspects of information protection. This does not mean responsibility for implementation but does mean strategic and functional leadership. Corporate security should manage development of the information security program in response to strategies approved by the information security committee or equivalent and policies that represent management's risk acceptance position.

Information Security Committee   The ISC is composed of representatives of the important functional and business organizations as appropriate to company organization and policy. The committee is responsible for identification of issues, development of strategies, and internal implementation of the agreed-upon information security policies and standards.

Information Security Managers   Information security managers are responsible for information security for an organizational element, as defined by the company.

Information System Managers   Information system managers are responsible for corporate-level data operations and networks. They implement the logical (i.e., hardware and software) security measures required by security standards.

Business Manager   Business managers at all levels are responsible for the security of all assigned assets, including information.

All Employees   All company employees accept information security as an integral part of their job assignments.

OUTPUT OF THE DEFENSIVE SET PROCESS

The completed Defensive Set process should produce the following:

- *Policies* are terse statements of management intent concerning information security. All players commit to policies.
- *Standards* support the policies with practical internal information security definitions, requirements, and processes. At the corporate level, standards should be limited to requirements that demand consistency throughout the company.
- *Commitments* obtained through the goals set process bind the various players to participation and contribution.

SUMMARY

The Defensive Set three-dimensional matrix is offered as a method for resolving complex issues concerning the establishment of information protection. The matrix approach should be useful in any information security effort.

12

Information Security Directives

The corporate information that spies seek appears in a number of forms, including computer-stored data, blueprints, letters or memoranda, files, formulas, charts and diagrams, production models and prototypes. Espionage also profits from visual observations and the interception of verbal communications. In effect, anything of corporate informational value becomes a potential industrial espionage target.

Norman R. Bottom and Robert R. J. Gallati, *Industrial Espionage*,
Butterworth, 1984, p. 5

When the number of company employees exceeds the fingers on a hand, a company needs instruction in writing, or directives, if the organization is to protect critical business information in an efficient and cost-effective manner. Information security directives typically consist of a company policy supported by a set of standards and, in some cases, procedures. This chapter addresses the justification for directives and presents an example of policies and standards.

Businesses need information security directives for the following reasons:

1. To establish a proprietary claim to information, the company must be prepared to show that it has done the following:

    *   Identified which information is valuable
    *   Established a process to protect it
    *   Trained and motivated employees to follow the process

    Properly written directives are the means for accomplishing the first and second tasks and are the basis for the third.
2. Effective protection requires that all employees in all departments, divisions, and geographic units follow information security rules. Directives are the only way to make this happen. They provide the basis for training and motivation, and consistency of action across the company.
3. Protection must apply to all information forms. Directives facilitate this consistency by defining the appropriate procedure for each environment or circumstance.

In this chapter a model policy and standard that support information security in a large company are presented, and the rationale is analyzed and explained.

DEFINITIONS FOR SECURITY DIRECTIVES

To develop good security policies, standards, and procedures and to ensure their optimal use, it is important that the parties involved agree on a set of definitions. This is good management, which applies to all business activities.

Policy. A concise statement of management position, intent, or principle. A policy should be tersely worded. A policy may identify responsibilities and may limit authority. A policy does not contain procedures and therefore should seldom need to be changed. A policy may stipulate that one or more standards are to be published to provide procedural instruction to be followed across the company. A policy includes a statement describing the objective and scope of the directive. The policy should provide a clear and concise explanation. Definitions and a list of supporting directives may be useful.

Standard. A detailed description of the requirements to be followed throughout the company. A primary purpose of a standard is consistency of action by all employees. Standards may provide procedures.

Procedure. An explanation of a series of actions or operations used in a local or divisional setting in support of a standard. An example is a standard that requires that data processing facilities be secured. Local procedures are needed to provide compliance with local laws. In some places armed guards are not permitted, whereas in other areas they may be required.

MODEL INFORMATION SECURITY DIRECTIVES

A fictitious company (ABCompany) is used to illustrate practical policy and standards concerning information security. Companies that have similar policies, classifications, and procedures include IBM Corporation, Xerox Corporation, Digital Equipment Corporation, and Union Carbide Corporation. Notes are provided where appropriate to clarify or emphasize important features of the directives.

POLICY

The following section provides an illustration of a properly constructed information protection policy for the fictitious ABCompany.

ABCompany Information Protection Policy Background

Information is ABCompany's most important business resource. Along with people, materials, parts and finished goods, facilities and equipment, and financial assets, information provides the means for business success. Uniquely among the resources listed, information provides ABCompany with a competitive edge.

Information is expensive to develop, process, deliver, and store. Information may be the only nonrecoverable asset; once information is exposed, it has lost confidentiality. Although legal redress may result in a monetary award, the information may no longer provide a competitive advantage. The loss or improper modification of information may also cause critical damage to the success of ABCompany in a highly competitive - industry.

Statement of Policy

This ABCompany information protection policy is intended to do the following:

1. Secure ABCompany information in an efficient manner that assures protection from unauthorized disclosure, destruction, or modification
2. Take all prudent measures to establish ABCompany's proprietary rights to important information and to allow an effective defense of those rights in a court of law, should such action be necessary

NOTE: The first section explains clearly why ABCompany is establishing an information security program. The second part is the statement of policy that underlies all following directives.

Scope

This policy applies to all employees of ABCompany, unless in conflict with local law, in which case the appropriate ABCompany manager must devise effective lawful processes to ensure equivalent protection.

NOTE: For a business operating internationally, it is important that policy provide an alternative for managers operating under laws that may be different from those in the United States and other developed countries.

Requirements

Information protection applies to ABCompany information in all forms—mental or orally delivered, electronic (machine-readable), and written (human-readable). The forms of information and the required marking and protective handling are described later in more detail in the "Information Protection Standards" section.

The effort expended on protection of ABCompany information is to be devised to minimize costs while best suiting the information's risk, value, or sensitivity, as indicated by the ABCompany information classification assigned by the responsible information owner or information custodian.

NOTE: The foregoing Requirements paragraphs establish the foundation for information security. Any effective protection effort rests on identification of which information elements are to be protected; protection of these elements in all forms in which they might occur; and investment in protective measures that reflect the risk acceptance posture of the company.

1. The risk, value, and sensitivity of a particular element of information is determined through the ABCompany information classification process. The ABCompany information classifications are as follows:

    Highest level
    ABCompany Restricted
    ABCompany Personal

    Middle level
    ABCompany Private

    ABCompany Security Standards establishes definitions, procedures for information classification, and resulting protection measures.

NOTE: More or fewer classifications may be appropriate in given circumstances. As a rule, fewer classifications facilitate management and lower the cost of administration.

2. Proper information classification is the responsibility of all ABCompany employees who are information originators, information owners, or information custodians. When routine business information has little risk associated with possible unauthorized disclosure, no ABCompany classification is required. However, all business information used in the course of ABCompany operations is considered private to ABCompany, and there is no blanket approval for outside release of information in any case.

NOTE: Paragraph 2 is based on the concept that information is always provided on a need-to-know basis. Hence, although most company information is not subjected to company classification, there is no implied right for anyone to expose business information without formal approval.

3. Information protection is the responsibility of all ABCompany employees. Certain specific responsibilities are defined in the standard. ABCompany information that has been company classified is protected as specified in the "Information Protection Standards" section.

NOTE: Paragraph 3 establishes a most important rule: Security is everyone's business. It sounds trite, but in today's communications-rich world, the participation of all employees is a necessity.

4. The requirements herein may apply to information entrusted to ABCompany by customers, suppliers, business partners, and individuals. However, if ABCompany is contractually obligated to follow other protection methods, or if government regulations apply, those should be observed.

NOTE: The business is legally obligated to establish procedures for protecting information belonging to others and identified as proprietary by the other party. Company legal counsel should define the meaning of this requirement in clearly set procedure.

Exception to Policy

ABCompany Security Standards provide that certain identified ABCompany managers may authorize alternative protection methods when business requirements so justify.

NOTE: Security always responds to business needs. Because business is the taking of risk, security measures must be flexible enough to allow management decisions about accepting defined risks or using alternative measures.

Supporting Responsibilities

ABCompany Security, through the divisional security functions, issues and maintains company security policies and monitors the effectiveness of information security.

The ABCompany Information Security Committee establishes information security program strategy, identifies information security issues and solutions, and commits to divisional implementation thereof.

NOTE: The two foregoing paragraphs delineate the company's information security management structure. This is a structure for a large business; smaller businesses would probably have simpler arrangements, but the same tasks apply.

ABCompany managers ensure that all employees are aware of and comply with ABCompany information security requirements as specified in the "Information Protection Standards" section.

NOTE: Getting middle management, which is usually beset by myriad problems, to take security seriously is a challenge. The policy establishes clearly the responsibility of management in the matter.

ABCompany audit and operational analysis monitors compliance with *Security Standards* and provides reports of same to the appropriate managers, per audit routine.

NOTE: The company auditors are the enforcement division. They are the means of making sure that managers follow policy.

Reference: See the "Information Protection Standards" section (see other references therein).

INFORMATION PROTECTION STANDARDS

Whereas policy provides a terse statement of management intent, standards provide the detailed instructions necessary to assure a cohesive, complete, and effective information protection program. An illustration of a model information security standard, with notes for the reader, follows.

ABCompany Security Standard Summary

This standard explains the requirements of ABCompany security policy for information protection and establishes procedures for the following:

- ABCompany information classification
- Marking, handling, storing, and delivering ABCompany classified information in all forms (mental, written, electronic)

Scope

This standard applies to all ABCompany organizations and employees, unless in conflict with law. In such case, the local ABCompany manager is responsible for devising equivalent protection methods under the Exception to Policy process herein.

Definitions

NOTE: It is important that terms be carefully defined. In many instances, employees may misunderstand instructions that appear clear to security professionals. For international business, great care must be taken to ensure that translations to other languages convey the intent of the original standard and are not simply literal translations.

Classification.   The process of assigning a defined term (the *classification*) as an indicator of value, sensitivity, or risk so as to establish the level of protection required for a specified element of information. Classification decisions are usually made by the information originator, information owner, or custodian. ABCompany has three information classifications. These are described in the section on Requirements.

Classification guide.   A tool to assist information originators or custodians in determining the appropriate ABCompany classification for an information file or document (see Appendix B).

Custodian.   The manager or administrator responsible for managing, processing, storing, or conserving a particular set of information. For example, a personnel administrator may maintain certain personnel records. The sponsor (see also *Information Owner*) of the application files in a computer system has a custodial responsibility. An employee who receives an ABCompany classified document, message, or verbal disclosure has custodial responsibility.

Disclosure.   The provision or showing of information to a person, organization, or system. Disclosure may be oral (meetings, telephone conversations, personal speech); by means of presentation of transparencies, charts, or 35-mm slides; by means of a computer system access or display; or by means of transfer of paper, including photographs.

Electronic information.   Information in digital, analog, or other machine-readable form.

Information form.   The manner in which information occurs. Information form is written (printed), electronic (machine readable), or mental. All forms must be protected as specified in the section on Requirements.

Information owner.   Usually the manager budgeting for an application or the senior manager of an organization that has primary responsibility for an element of information. For example, the vice-president for personnel is the information owner for personnel records.

Mental information.   Company classified information provided to an employee by means of verbal discussion, documents, transparencies or slides, pictures, or other media in the course of assigned job duties. Each employee must complete a contractual obligation at the time of hire or contract. This agreement is usually a disclosure agreement that binds the employee not to use the information in any manner, place, or time not authorized by ABCompany.

Need to know.   The basis for information protection. A rule that establishes that an ABCompany employee's or trusted contractor's privilege to see, modify, move, or delete ABCompany classified information is not a right and is limited by policy. Such privileges, if any, are based solely on the employee's or contractor's job assignment.

NOTE: Need to know is an extremely important concept. Some employees, especially in paternalistic companies, may believe they have an inherent right to know everything. This rule establishes that any information rights granted are privileges related to job assignments.

Originator.   The company employee who prepares or authenticates the initial information file or document. Such files, documents, or oral disclosures may be new information, revisions of old information, compilations of several elements of information, or merely copies of information prepared by others but presented in a new context.

Proprietary information.   Any information the company believes to have a value or sensitivity or that may pose a risk if disclosed, justifying a claim to proprietary or trade secret rights. In ABCompany such information is referred to as *ABCompany Classified* (see Appendixes A and B).

Written information.   Human-readable information in written, printed, or symbolic forms on paper, plastic (transparencies, slides), or microforms or in photographs or other physical media.

Information Protection Requirements

ABCompany regards all business-related information as private and not for release. Certain critical business information is identified as requiring special protection efforts by means of assignment and marking of an ABCompany information classification. The protection requirements specified herein apply to all information forms (mental, written, and electronic).

All disclosure of ABCompany business information to ABCompany employees is based on need to know as defined earlier.

ABCompany employees have no inherent right to company information. Information privileges (to see, move, modify, disclose, or delete ABCompany classified information) are based on employee job assignments. All ABCompany employees, as a condition of employment, must sign a disclosure agreement. The form of agreement suitable for any individual employee or situation is determined by ABCompany legal counsel.

NOTE: A disclosure agreement, also called a nondisclosure agreement, forms a contract in which a trusted person agrees to hold confidential and not use for any forbidden or unintended purposes information provided in the course of employment or during and after other business relationships. This agreement is essential if the company is to be able to defend its rights to proprietary information.

The disclosure of ABCompany business information to outsiders (non-ABCompany parties who may be suppliers, contractors, marketers, advertising agencies, and so forth) requires contractual disclosure agreements, as determined by ABCompany legal counsel.

NOTE: In today's business environment, outsiders such as suppliers, customers, consultants, and business partners often require electronic connections to company networks and computers. Electronic data interchange (EDI) systems illustrate such requirements. A careful and thorough procedure is necessary to ensure that the connection is business justified and the connection does not pose an unacceptable security risk.

Classification of Information

When the value, sensitivity, or risk associated with ABCompany information justifies a protection effort, ABCompany information classification indicates the level of protection to be provided. ABCompany managers must ensure that any information for which an identifiable risk, sensitivity, or value is evident is promptly subjected to ABCompany information classification (see Appendix B for detailed guidance).

Routine business information that has little or no risk associated with possible disclosure need not be assigned a company classification. However, because all ABCompany business information must be considered private to the company, such unclassified information should not be publicly disclosed without proper ABCompany approval from the originator or information owner. In addition, approvals may be required from the public relations department. ABCompany legal counsel can provide guidance.

NOTE: Decisions on public release of information always involve questions of propriety, responsibility, competitive effect, proprietary rights of the company or others, and similar questions. No employee should ever announce or provide company information (anything used inside the company for business purposes) without review and approval. Further, a formal process should be at hand for review of technical and professional papers proposed by employees for public presentation.

Prompt and timely ABCompany information classification is essential at origination, compilation, or modification of information. Classification is the basis for ensuring the correct protection of information—in a computer file, document, or mental disclosure—at all times during the useful life of the information.

NOTE: Suitable protection follows from classification. When no classification is provided, the information is not protected because users and recipients may not recognize the value or sensitivity of the information.

Special Situations

ABCompany may have a contractual obligation to protect information supplied to it by customers, contractors, suppliers, or individuals. In such cases, it may be appropriate to assign a company classification of *Private* to the information while it is in ABCompany custody to ensure protection.

If ABCompany information is provided to contractors, customers, or other non-ABCompany parties, the information may require a *Proprietary* or *Confidential* notice and in some cases must also be subjected to company information classification. The advice of ABCompany legal counsel should be obtained in such cases.

ABCompany Classification

It is impossible to provide a comprehensive, accurate list of the titles of documents and files that fall in a particular classification. Titles of reports and files vary among ABCompany organizations and locations. Classification always relies on the learned judgment of the originator, custodian, or senior manager of the originating organization (see Appendix B).

The ABCompany information classifications are as follows:

ABCompany Restricted

ABCompany Personal

ABCompany Private

Restricted and *Personal* identify information that has the highest relative level of risk, sensitivity, or value associated with unauthorized disclosure, destruction, or modification. Information assigned to either of these ABCompany classes may be provided only to individuals who are identified, by name, by the originator or custodian and whose job assignment justifies such disclosure. Information in these classifications requires special distribution and handling (see Marking and Handling).

Restrictions for *ABCompany Restricted* and *Personal*

If transparencies, 35-mm slides, and microforms are to display *ABCompany Restricted* information, the following requirements apply:

1. The originator of the information, information owner, or custodian must approve a list of attendees, by name and in writing, before the meeting
2. A record of those shown the information must be maintained similar to that required for the distribution of written materials.

NOTE: Business people often use transparencies or 35-mm slides in meetings at which the presenter has only a cursory awareness of the identities and jobs of the audience. Such a circumstance violates the need-to-know principle. As a rule, if information is assigned one of the higher classifications, it is not suitable for a presentation unless the audience is restricted (for example, the board of directors or executive committee).

Information classified *ABCompany Restricted* might apply to information that has high risk or sensitivity. Examples are business plans, new product plans, plans concerning the purchase of businesses or transactions concerning real estate, unannounced strategic business reorganization plans, and unannounced financial summaries.

Information properly classified *ABCompany Personal* includes any information a typical individual would keep confidential, or which by law or prudent decision of the originator should be kept confidential. Such information may include job performance appraisals, payroll records, health records, and personnel records. *ABCompany Personal* information may be made available only to the subject employee, the immediate supervisor, an ABCompany hiring manager (with employee's permission), the administrator of the servicing personnel activity, legal counsel, audit and operational analysis department when required for assigned duties, and corporate security.

NOTE: In some cases, it may be appropriate to use *ABCompany Personal* in conjunction with another ABCompany class. An example is a case in which a senior executive is offered a transfer. The details of the transfer might be classified *ABCompany Restricted* until announced, and the pay and benefits associated with the move (which could be in the same document) might be classified *ABCompany Personal*. In such cases, both classes should be shown, and the more restrictive protection requirement applies.

Information that has moderate risk, sensitivity, or value should be classified *ABCompany Private*. Information classified as *ABCompany Private* includes documents and computer files such as customer lists, product delivery schedules, prospects lists, competitive survey data, designs, individual organizational or financial plans, and security plans. *ABCompany Private* information may be shared with groups of employees or contractors on the basis of their job assignments and need to know.

NOTE: This classification is intended for information to be provided to groups of employees, such as those assigned a project or a common task. Compare this classification with *Restricted*, which indicates that the information so classified is addressed to named individuals only. This is a critical concept; it is important that it be understood.

Marking Requirements

All ABCompany information subjected to company classification, whether in written, printed, pictorial, microform, or electronic form, must be marked plainly and in such a manner as to be evident at first glance. The ABCompany classification logo, by means of a stamp or computer graphic, is the preferred method for marking. However, the following special instructions provide for marking of documents when a stamp or graphic logo is not available.

Each copy of an *ABCompany Restricted* document must be assigned a number, to be entered on the first page of the document in the lower right-hand corner. This copy number is to be entered on the Log and Cover Sheet (see Appendix C), which shows the addressee to whom each copy is assigned. If the information is in electronic form, the Log and Cover Sheet (see "Handling Requirements" later in this chapter) is a header with similar information and also must show the copy number assigned to each addressee.

Paper Documents   All ABCompany classified documents must be marked with the assigned ABCompany classification at the bottom of all pages. The ABCompany classification stamp should be used. This requirement includes transparencies, 35-mm slides, drawings, and pictures.

Magnetic or Other Electronically Readable Media, Including but Not Restricted to Tapes and Disks
All such media must be marked with the appropriate ABCompany classification in a clear manner obvious to people using the media.

Electronic Forms   Files or documents in electronic form must be clearly marked with the assigned ABCompany classification, if practical in the same manner as paper documents, using the graphic ABCompany classification logo. If graphics are not available on the computer system being used, the ABCompany classification should be typed at the bottom of the page, spaced away from the text or data, and marked with asterisks to highlight the classification as follows:

*****ABCompany PRIVATE*****

When or if printed from a computer system, these markings suffice, and additional logo stamps are not required.

NOTE: When properly developed for computer systems, information classification markings should be commonly available from computer graphics files and should emulate the design of the classification logo used on printed paper or rubber stamps.

Should the marking of electronic messages, reports, etc., at the bottom of each page be impractical, the classification marking should appear at important places throughout the file or document, such as at paragraph headings, and at the end.

NOTE: The foregoing paragraph accommodates a deficiency in office system design in that such systems may not allow for graphic marking of the classification logo.

Microforms must be marked with the ABCompany classification so as to be noticed by the human eye without magnification.

Handling Requirements

ABCompany Restricted   Must have a Log and Cover sheet (see Appendix C) that indicates the title, date, addressees, copy number sent to each, and originator. This requirement also applies to electronic documents or files, for which the originator may prepare a header with similar information and markings, in any convenient form. The Log and Cover sheet is an integral part of the file or document, and is retained by the originator as a record of distribution.

Must be mailed in double envelopes. The internal envelope is to be marked with the ABCompany classification "To be opened by addressee only." The outer envelope must be opaque and sealed. The outer envelope is to have only the name and address of the authorized recipient.

May not be copied or duplicated without the written permission of the originator. May not be forwarded electronically.

May not be sent over networks unless encrypted. *ABCompany Restricted* information should not be stored for extended periods on network-accessible (on-line) computers or disks unless encrypted.

Must not be distributed by means of facsimile unless encrypted.

May be sent through First Class mail with double envelope as indicated earlier. Receipts are optional at discretion of the originator.

ABCompany Personal   Must be mailed in double envelopes. These envelopes are to be addressed, marked, and handled the same as for *ABCompany Restricted* distribution. Log and Cover Sheet is not required.

Must not be sent over networks unless encrypted.

Must not be sent by means of facsimile unless the identified recipient is standing by at the receiving machine and the information is encrypted while on network circuits.

ABCompany Private   Must be mailed in double envelopes. These envelopes are to be addressed, marked, and handled the same as for *ABCompany Restricted*. Log and Cover Sheet is not required.

May be sent over networks with appropriate message or document ABCompany classification marking.

Storage

ABCompany Restricted materials (e.g., papers, microforms, slides and transparencies, floppy disks, tapes) must be stored in a file cabinet equipped with a bar lock or safe. These materials should not be stored for extended periods of time on network-accessible disks unless encrypted.

ABCompany Personal or *ABCompany Private* materials (e.g., papers, microforms, slides and transparencies, floppy disks, tapes) must be stored in a locked desk or file cabinet.

NOTE: When volume prevents storage as prescribed, a secure area may be established to restrict access to those authorized. Information retention or backup requirements may require such an area to be a vault with fire-resistant construction.

Destruction

All ABCompany classified materials (including paper, microforms, slides and transparencies) must be destroyed by shredding or by depositing in ABCompany classified waste containers for controlled collection and certified destruction. Magnetic media (tapes, disks, cartridges) must be thoroughly degaussed or written over so as to destroy readable data thereon. Magnetic media that contain or have contained *ABCompany Restricted* information should be burned or otherwise destroyed so as to be unusable.

Clean Desk

ABCompany information security procedures are intended to provide reasonable protection to ABCompany classified information while keeping interference with business operations at a minimum.

In general, employees are expected to log off systems and lock up all ABCompany classified information if they are to be away from the workplace for two hours or more.

ABCompany employees should be alert to possible exposure of ABCompany classified information should an office or area be completely vacated for even a brief period of time.

NOTE: This is a difficult rule to enforce, but until it is followed, the company cannot assume that the information protection program is effective. What use is it to invest in sophisticated information security methods if employees do not take the simple precaution of locking up valuable information?

Exception to Policy

Should ABCompany business requirements justify alternative means to protect ABCompany classified information, an Exception to Policy approval may be obtained, as follows:

For *ABCompany Restricted* and *ABCompany Personal* information, exception must be justified by a risk-cost analysis that shows the vulnerability of the information and the cost of complying with the standard as opposed to another method of protection. The exception approval must be signed by an ABCompany corporate vice president, and the director of security must concur and maintain the approval documents for audit.

For *ABCompany Private* information, exception must be approved in writing by a division vice president. The division security manager maintains the approval for audit.

Responsibilities

Corporate Security   Throughout all divisions, establishes and monitors overall ABCompany information security programs. Assists ABCompany organizations with awareness and training requirements.

ABCompany Executive Security Board   Recommends policies necessary to address ABCompany information security vulnerabilities. Resolves company-wide security issues.

ABCompany Information Security Committee   Establishes information security strategies for ABCompany, identifies and resolves issues, develops solutions, and commits to worldwide implementation of agreed-upon solutions.

All ABCompany Managers   Protect ABCompany information through proper information classification, implementation of access controls, marking, handling, and storage procedures as specified in this standard, and continued employee awareness training. Institute appropriate local controls to ensure continuing compliance with this standard.

Information security should be considered an integral part of every employee's job responsibilities.

Division Security Managers   Publish supporting information security procedures appropriate to business requirements. Provide for employee awareness and training.

Site Security Managers or Coordinators   Provide local procedures and resources for proper protection, storage, and destruction of ABCompany classified information. Perform periodic surveys or audits to determine effectiveness. Maintain records of information destruction as locally appropriate. Supervise and monitor contracted information-destruction services. Support organizational requirements for employee training and awareness. Establish a process to report security violations.

All Employees   Are responsible for security awareness and compliance with this standard. As a condition of employment agree to protect ABCompany classified information and not to disclose any ABCompany classified information except as authorized. Responsible for reporting information security violations to their organizational security manager.

Audit and Operational Analysis   Monitors the general state of awareness and compliance with this standard.

References: *ABCompany Information Protection Policy*

Appendix A: ABCompany Information Universe

ABCompany considers all information used in the course of business operations to be private to the company. However, certain information is especially valuable or sensitive. This information is classified and is considered *proprietary*, or worth protecting. The Information Universe illustrates the value of company information and shows protection methods that can be used individually or together to provide security and to establish ABCompany's legal rights (see Figure 1–1).

Appendix B: ABCompany Information Classification Guide

The Classification Guide provides a simple indication intended to assist employees faced with information classification decisions. The following questions should guide ABCompany classification decisions but are never a substitute for good judgment based on knowledge of ABCompany business requirements.

1. What distribution would be appropriate considering the sensitivity of this information?
2. What value does this information have in light of its importance to ABCompany? Compare to other information that has already been classified.
3. Is this information more or less sensitive than other information that has been classified?
4. What risk is evident should this information be exposed?

Using the Classification Guide   An ABCompany employee making a classification decision should use the Guide while applying learned judgment. All four criteria do not necessarily apply in every case.

1. Distribution appropriate to sensitivity

   Only a few recipients as identified by the originator. Classify as *ABCompany Restricted.*
   Employees in a unit, project, office. Classify as *ABCompany Private.*
   All employees (published material). No classification.

2. Value assumed for the information

   Critical effect on ABCompany business if exposed. Classify as *ABCompany Restricted.*
   Could affect ABCompany's business to some degree if exposed. Classify as *ABCompany Private.*

3. Sensitivity of the information

   If revealed could subject ABCompany to severe embarrassment. Classify as *ABCompany Restricted.*
   If revealed could expose ABCompany plans or strategies. Classify as *ABCompany Private.*

4. Risk of use of the information

   If revealed could seriously damage business potential. Classify as *ABCompany Restricted.*
   If revealed could affect some ABCompany operations. Classify as *ABCompany Private.*

NOTE: *ABCompany Personal* is a special case (see *ABCompany Security Standards: Information Protection*).

Appendix C

********** **ABCompany RESTRICTED** **********

LOG AND COVER SHEET

Instructions: Originator completes and maintains with document file copy. Attach a copy to top of each document sent. If electronic distribution: (1) type facsimile of this log as first page of message, and (2) print document and file this log with it. Recipient acknowledges receipt if so requested (by phone or message). Cover remains affixed to top of document.

Document title: _____

Originator: _____

Date: _____ Document No. (optional) _____

Acknowledgment requested YES _____ NO _____ Written YES _____ NO _____

Addressees of this document: Copy No.:

_____

_____

_____

13

Establishing an Information Security Program

Many security managers and system managers assume they know how to establish an information security program. Unfortunately, many of these people find themselves starting over after problems develop. The following case illustrates the point.

Case

The information systems vice president of a large company decided that information was at risk. A member of the information system staff, with help from others, initiated an information protection program. After a considerable effort that lasted about two years, the company auditors reported that other staff groups and the operating units were not following the security requirements, which they regarded as a "systems matter."

Getting started correctly is critical. The following are steps for beginning a program:

1. Compose a team to develop and publish the company's information security classification nomenclature and definitions (see chapter 11). This same group can also write company information security policy. Team members should include company security managers, legal counsel, and administration.
2. Obtain corporate approval of the policy. In many companies, there is no established process, and an ad hoc effort is necessary. The team may have to determine the process for obtaining approval of the standards, when appropriate (see 3).
3. Establish a team to write the information protection standards. Chapter 12 offers examples. Team members should include representatives from security, legal counsel, personnel, information systems, and important operating groups, among others, to suit company practices.
4. Establish training programs to educate employees about information security requirements. Pamphlets and posters are useful in disseminating the message to employees.
5. Arrange for information security matters to be a part of all routine company audits.

OBTAINING SUPPORT FROM SENIOR MANAGEMENT

Unless they are properly advised by expert security managers, most business executives seldom understand security issues. Because security is not one of their primary concerns (and probably should not be), executives typically deal with security for exceptions or incident by incident. This style of management has the following two unfortunate effects:

1. The senior executive may view security as a single-issue management concern. In other words, if recent property thefts have been addressed, the executive may see company security as having only one responsibility—for resolving that situation.
2. Senior management may see security as a purely responsive activity, with no strategic responsibility. In this case, the executives expect security to respond to emergencies but have no vision of the necessary and prudent planning needed for effective security management.

A primary responsibility of the company security director or security manager is to provide this strategic view for senior management. By offering executive management a concise overview of societal and business environments that give rise to security threats and vulnerabilities, the security director should establish the basis for long-range security strategy. This strategy underlies security investment, effective security organization, and proper assignment of security responsibilities.

The security manager must direct the attention of senior management to the strategic decisions needed for continued security protection for the critical resources of the business. Information is among the most important of these resources.

Case

In a large multinational company, the talent and effort available for providing information security were devoted solely to computer security. Operating management was extremely concerned about vulnerabilities relating to computers and networks. At the same time, senior executive management was concerned about repeated leaks to the press concerning strategic business decisions. These leaks almost always involved the passing of papers. The information security effort was not reconciled with the business risks but was tied up in technologically interesting matters.

An information security effort without strategy and continually involved with addressing emergencies as they arise is doomed to deliver poor value and to cost the company more in the long run. Money and effort may be directed at matters that have little bearing on the protection of the company's critical information.

Information protection strategy implies the correct assignment of information security responsibility. The subject is not one that can be dealt with on a cursory or casual basis. Information security is a complex subject the mastery of which requires considerable experience and in-depth knowledge concerning the practical, technical, and legal aspects described in this book. An incorrect or inadequate assignment of the company information security responsibilities can mean that limited resources may be misdirected or wasted. Information security is not simple and evident any more than safety or good facility management are plain common sense.

The company information protection manager should report to the director of security or to another senior manager, such as the auditing manager. The job should never be in the information system department.

DEFINING INFORMATION SECURITY IN TERMS OF MANAGEABILITY

Unless a subject can be defined, that is, boundaries can be drawn around it and its constituent parts identified, the subject cannot be managed. In the case of information security, the definition often seems to be in the eyes of the beholder. A lack of a crisp definition can compromise information security efforts.

The business enterprise view (Figure 13–1) gives an orderly and relatively precise picture of information security in relation to the overall protection of business resources. The business enterprise view is the correct view from the company director of security. In the establishment of a company information security program, it is absolutely essential that the managers planning the function have a clear view of its relationships with other security functions and thus with other parts of the company.

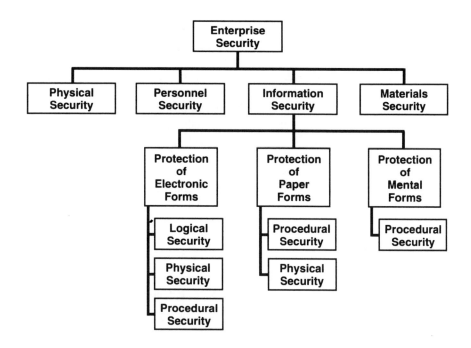

Figure 13–1   Enterprise view of security.

Some broad guidelines to consider when planning an information security program are as follows:

- Information security responds to business needs. The challenge is to provide the proper security at an acceptable cost, given the environment, risks, and available funds.
- Information security involves the protection of an intangible asset. Many traditional security approaches may not apply. Legal nuances, details of handling and marking, and other fairly esoteric matters may be essential.
- For many companies, information is the most critical business resource. Competitive position, market share, and profitability may depend on information generation and confidentiality. Protecting information in such a case is then a primary responsibility of the senior security manager.
- Information is among the most expensive and perishable of business resources. Many technology-oriented businesses spend 5–7 percent of revenue on generation, delivery, and use of information. Exposed information may not be recoverable.

THE BUSINESS ENTERPRISE VIEW OF SECURITY

The enterprise view provides managers with an understanding of the varied but interrelated responsibilities of company security. Unfortunately, many businesses continue to regard information protection as a mysterious technical matter that involves encryption and passwords and hence is outside the realm of company security. In fact, information protection has much in common with traditional security matters. Effective information protection requires that information security be part of the senior security manager's overall responsibility for protecting the business.

The enterprise view shows that company security is responsible for protecting reputation, employees and visitors, plant, equipment, financial resources and materials, and information. There is some overlap among these responsibilities.

The information resource is an intangible asset that occurs in three general forms— mental, paper, and electronic. Consistent with the enterprise view of security that is responsive to business needs, a well-conceived information security program provides protection for all three forms. This protection must be consistent and balanced in relation to the vulnerabilities of and threats to each form and the limited security investment available.

PROGRAM GOALS

To be effective, an information security plan must have clearly established goals. For most companies, the following goals are defined by evident business requirements and court precedents:

Goal 1.   To prevent unauthorized disclosure, modification, or destruction of information and to assure reliable information services

Goal 2.   To establish the means for a successful claim to proprietary rights to information in a court of law, should such action be appropriate.

COMPONENTS OF INFORMATION SECURITY

Given the enterprise view and the program goals, the components of a comprehensive information security program can be defined. The work occurs in categories defined as *administrative* (procedural work), *physical* (facility protection work), and *logical* (work involving the selection, development, and application of computer software and hardware).

An important responsibility relative to each of the work categories is training and motivation. As noted earlier, having "most" employees protect information is not good enough. In most businesses, about one-third of employees know and follow the information protection rules. Another one-third know there are rules but may not be sure about exactly what to do. The last third either know nothing about information security or are simply not motivated to follow the prescribed security practices.

INFORMATION CLASSIFICATION: THE FOUNDATION

Administrative work includes the foundation for any information security effort—information classification. Company information classification identifies which information is valuable or sensitive and allows responsible security managers to make appropriate decisions about security investments (see chapters 5 and 12). Defining and planning company information classification is the first step in initiating information protection. All activities and requirements follow from proper information classification.

INFORMATION SECURITY WORK AND FORMS OF INFORMATION

It may be helpful in the planning of an information security program to consider information security work categories in relation to all forms of information. All the work elements must be *assigned* as responsibilities. No responsibilities can be assumed to be met. Table 13–1 shows information security work in relation to all forms of information. The paper form includes documents, microforms, transparencies, photographs, and other human-readable information presentations. Chapter 11 provides guidance in this work.

CONTENT OF THE INFORMATION SECURITY
WORK CATEGORIES

Mental Information

Mental information refers to the job-related knowledge employees acquire during their time with the company. This information may be passed orally, read from reports or plans, or read from computer displays. In any case, every employee gains a great deal

Table 13–1   Information Security Work in Relation to All Forms of Information

Security Level	Information Form		
	Mental	*Electronic*	*Paper*
Procedural	Contracts	Access authority (grant and deny)	Access authority (grant and deny)
Physical		Protection of computer infrastructure	Protection of document infrastructure (limit access on basis of right to know)
Logical		Control of access to electronic forms (on basis of need to know)	

of mental information during his or her work experience. Some of this information is valuable and may be considered proprietary. The company security manager is responsible for working with company legal counsel and personnel administrators to establish contractual controls that ensure extended protection of this information. Usually this is done through disclosure clauses in employment contracts.

Electronic Information

Electronic forms of information are protected with security elements in all three work categories. Most security failures with regard to electronic forms of information are the result of lax administration. Skilled computer experts who decide to attack the company are a threat, but most losses occur because of a failure in a relatively simple administrative responsibility, such as not cancelling the password of a transferred or terminated employee.

Administrative   Administrative procedures identify sensitive information and establish the privileges of employees to access such information. Such privileges must always be based on need to know and never on individual curiosity or organizational relationships. Usually these access authorities are managed through access-control lists established by information owners and administered by computer security specialists. The information owner is usually the functional manager responsible for the information in question. For example, the vice-president or personnel manager may be the information owner for personnel data files.

> **Data-processing or information system managers should never be data owners and should never act as the privilege-granting authority.**

Logical Logical security measures involve installation and operation of computer security software and hardware (often called *tools*) that control access, monitor activities, report anomalies, and react to threats. Logical security processes should provide support for appropriate marking, handling, and delivery of company classified information in electronic forms. In most cases, the services provided by logical security are defined in information security standards, and the software and hardware that delivers these services are selected and maintained by the information system organization. The information protection manager need not be a technical expert with knowledge of all the hardware and software used, but he or she should have enough knowledge to ascertain that the security services meet the company's standards.

Physical Physical security measures protect the information infrastructure, which may include the office and its computers, copiers, facsimile machines, file cabinets and vaults; copy centers; data centers; communication centers; and network facilities. Any space that contains electronic gear should be secured and must never be used for unrelated purposes. One calls to mind the ubiquitous use of communication wiring closets to store brooms and mops.

Paper-based Information

Protection of paper forms of information requires security elements from the administrative and physical work categories.

Administrative Administrative work to protect information on paper includes authorization to use information as appropriate to job assignment. The need-to-know principle is always important but is especially critical for document control. No employee has a right to see any information. Rather, the employee is given a privilege to access information only because of a job assignment. There are no other acceptable justifications. Company procedures should be such that disclosure of the highest classification of information is controlled to limit disclosure to the absolute minimum number of people. Marking, storage, delivery, and destruction procedures are a part of administrative information protection.

Physical Physical protection of information on paper includes secure handling and storage facilities, secure destruction facilities and processes, secure office workstations, access control for facilities, and similar measures. The tasks for physical protection of information on paper in many cases are the same as for electronic forms of information.

LEGAL ASPECTS OF INFORMATION SECURITY

So far this discussion has concerned information protection measures intended to support Goal 1, that is, preventing unauthorized disclosure, modification, or destruction of information and assuring continued reliable information services. Goal 2, assuring that the company can make a successful defense of proprietary claims, requires additional effort. In general, courts have held that certain conditions must exist for a successful claim to ownership of information. There are two sets of requirements—those related to the information itself and those related to the information security program.

1. Required information precautions
    To be considered proprietary (or trade secret), information must be shown to have met the following measures:

    a. The information must have been closely held, that is, not generally known, even within the company.
    b. The information can be proved to have commercial value, that is, the company's exclusive knowledge of the information may be demonstrated to be a prerequisite to profit.

    These requirements illustrate the fact that much information typically found in business operations cannot, in any case, be claimed as proprietary. There is little purpose in expending security resources on such information. Proper classification is the key to sifting out the information that does not justify protection.

2. Required information security program accomplishments
    To prove that information is closely held, court precedent (case law) seems to require demonstration of all of the following three elements:

    a. The company must have identified which information is sensitive or valuable. (This is the all-important classification process.)
    b. The company must have established procedures for identifying and protecting such information in normal business operation.
    c. The company's employees must follow such procedures as a matter of course during routine business operation. (Testimony to the effect that managers regard information security cavalierly or disregard it entirely can compromise a company's claim to proprietary rights, even if the other requirements are met.)

A failure of training or motivation or both, often as a result of laxity on the part of middle management, forms the shoals upon which many legal claims founder.

Before starting to work on information security, one should consider the Enterprise View. This might include the following:

*   Computer security is a subset of information security. By itself, computer security does not protect information, which occurs more frequently in other forms. A 1990 study purported to show that information risks, in order of severity, were the following:

    1. Loose talk
    2. Careless paper handling
    3. Attacks on computer systems.[1]

- Information security is a primary responsibility of the business security department. All resources of a company are protected by the security department or its equivalent. Information is an important resource. Security of information should be assigned to protection professionals.
- A correct view of information security is essential to the development of an effective program. Important related responsibilities must be assigned.
- There are important business and legal reasons for company investment in a quality information security program. These may not be obvious. It is extremely risky to implement a security program without understanding all the requirements (see chapter 11).

SECURITY ORGANIZATION AS A MIRROR OF BUSINESS STRATEGY

The security organization should reflect executive management's strategy in regard to risk taking. Many businesses have a security program without management commitment. Executives may believe security is trivial or unimportant, but most are afraid to do without it. Neatly uniformed guards may provide a warm feeling. But really effective security—at an acceptable cost—requires skilled security professionals who understand the company's business.

Business managers who defer all security strategy and then panic at the first emergency are like householders who put the cheapest locks on their doors. No one can say that security was ignored, but there is little protection. After the burglar has visited, criticism of the security effort is easy, but the lack of accepted management responsibility—and security strategy—has had painful results.

Effective security, which returns the most protection for the investment, requires proper organization and assignment of responsibility. Each major class of asset perceived to have a value and a vulnerability associated with it must be clearly and unambiguously assigned a security function. Although the asset protection classes may vary among industries, general classes are as follows.

Personnel   Employees are subject to many risks at the workplace, on company property, and when traveling on business. The company should provide suitable protection for key employees when prudence so dictates. The working environment must be secured from unwarranted risks. At a minimum, members of the public should not be permitted casual access to company facilities. Medical and other emergency services are usually a part of the security "envelope" provided to employees at work.

Facilities   Factories, warehouses, laboratories, offices, and other facilities have intrinsic value and contain an array of expensive equipment, products, or raw materials. To safeguard these physical assets, the company should limit access to people who require entry for business purposes. Fencing, electronic surveillance, and lighting systems may be needed.

Materials, Parts, Components, and Finished Goods   These commodities may be in manufacturing, in storage, in transit between processes, en route from suppliers, or on the way to customers as sold goods. There are obvious vulnerabilities to theft or diversion, damage, or loss. Many companies have almost no control over goods, even high-cost goods. At minimum, the security program should provide identification and tracking of high-cost or sensitive items. In some cases, such as retail shopping areas, this includes surveillance of the public and may necessitate controls for high-value assets, such as product tagging.

Information   Information is the only intangible asset on the list, and therefore is among the most difficult to secure. From a strategic point of view, the form of information (written, electronic, mental) should make little difference in security investment decisions. Loss of or damage to one form may be as bad as loss of or damage to any other. At minimum, the company should know which elements of information are critical to business success and should make carefully considered strategic decisions concerning protection of those elements. There are business and legal reasons for protecting information. Information protection is a complex and difficult issue that cannot be dealt with in a cursory manner.

UNDERSTANDING MANAGEMENT'S RISK ACCEPTANCE POSTURE

Management's decisions concerning acceptance of risks involve selection from a range of alternatives. Because business is a taking of risk in the hope of a resulting profit, risk is an integral part of business. The security manager's role is to assist management in controlling risks, especially those management considers unacceptable. However, the security manager must have in mind that security solutions are only one choice from a menu from which management may choose.

The means for dealing with business risks include the following:

- Changing to alternative methods, processes, or procedures is a business decision that may eliminate the need for security.
- Buying insurance (i.e., sharing risk with others) can be a hedge against failure of a security effort.
- Installing security protection is the most obvious way to try to control risk and limit the effect of realized threats.
- Accepting risks as a cost of doing business (self-insurance) is an alternative in which a company's experience convinces management that the potential loss can be managed. An example is self-insurance by a company with a large fleet of trucks.

Management's decision to select security protection as a risk control measure should be implemented through a formal security program. *Formal* means that management's risk-taking posture is expressed through published policies and standards. Information security policies should be written to recognize that business is essentially a taking of risks. A security program that is tailored to business needs allows for controlled management decisions to take risks. Chapter 12 illustrates security directives that provide for exceptions concerning acceptance of risks.

THE SECURITY DIRECTIVES STRUCTURE

After the information classification structure has been designed, policies and standards should be written.

The parts of an effective directives structure are policies, standards, and local procedures. *Policies* provide a terse, succinct statement of management intent. Policies state *what* is to be accomplished. Well-written policies should seldom if ever have to be changed, because they contain no procedure. A useful rule is that a policy should never exceed both sides of one sheet of paper. Otherwise, it probably includes procedures and must be revised frequently as business methods and environments change.

Policy always applies to the entire company, without exception. If a policy is not suited for a division, group, or geographic entity of the business, it has probably not been written succinctly enough to include only limiting policy statements appropriate to the subject.

Standards establish the minimum actions necessary to meet policy and to ensure consistency. Standards provide for variations in implementation of policy by allowing latitude for local procedures. Standards state *how* managers and employees are to comply with policy. Different standards can be developed to address security requirements for organizational units or functions. Different standards are appropriate only (1) if business operations dictate a need for unique security processes and (2) if varying the standard does not violate wise business practices or create security vulnerabilities in interfaces between units or functions.

Local procedures are additive to standards. They allow for facility or functional requirements that address local situations. Procedures usually relate to specific, individual job assignments (for example, how to register classified documents at a location or how to log tape library activities).

As a rule, security decisions should be made at the lowest practical level, given the company's needs for strategy, economy, and consistency. In other words, policy should avoid setting detailed requirements, and standards should avoid setting processes that impose unrealistic demands on local managers.

Chapter 12 provides definitions of policies and standards and offers a detailed model of security directives.

SETTING POLICY

What does management really want? Because management often does not understand the information security problem, it is difficult to determine just what is desired. Before a proposal for information security policy is developed, the security director or the executive charged with establishment of the program should provide senior executives with simple, realistic information about the risks involved and then should offer a range of options for investment in information security. The Defensive Set process described in Chapter 11 is a way to gain agreement before initiating a bid for executive support.

Although the security director may want to make a recommendation, the presentation of options helps develop a sense of appreciation for the business security situation. Security managers do not wish to be perceived as doom-and-gloom prophets. A calm and reasoned approach that begins with a consideration of risks and mentions alternative solutions and costs provides a business-decision basis for the discussion, a presentation style with which senior managers should be comfortable.

A proposal for information security investment could include alternatives such as the following:

- No investment. The company is willing to risk exposure, modification, or loss of information. The business effects or liabilities of any or all such incidents, were they to occur given the probabilities identified, are not considered worth the cost of an effective program.
- Selective protection and limited investment. The company is willing to accept risks of information exposure, unauthorized modification, or loss in all but a few carefully defined cases. In certain industries (e.g., the grocery industry) only personnel data may be considered sensitive enough to warrant protection.
- General protection with limited investment. This is the most usual case. The company is unwilling to accept the general classes of information risk. It decides to identify which information is sensitive or valuable and to direct protection investment to the most critical areas.

Case

A large, worldwide electronics manufacturer appointed a new security director, who was told to build a security program. The director offered the company's executive committee three alternatives, each differing in cost by one order of magnitude. At the low end was a program of security posters. At the high end was a full security effort. The executive committee chose the most expensive option after being briefed on potential risks and liabilities. There was no doubt about management commitment.

STATING THE "WHAT" OF INFORMATION SECURITY

Policy states the general intent of management with regard to the subject of the policy. A policy statement for information security might be as follows:

Information in all forms (written, electronic, mental) will be protected as appropriate for the value or sensitivity indicated by company information classification.

The policy may also stipulate and define the company's information classification terms. For example, the company's information classification is as follows:

Company Restricted. Information of the highest value or sensitivity, that deals with critical business strategy or product planning or other matters, and that if exposed or abused could cause serious harm to competitive position or embarrassment to the company, its officers, directors, or employees.

Company Private. Information with moderate value, that deals with ongoing business operations, and that if exposed or abused could cause loss of profits, business opportunity, or competitive position.

Company Personal. Information concerning people and that individuals would normally not wish to have disclosed to others.

The foregoing paragraphs constitute a complete policy statement. The policy does not address *how* but only *what*. The policy establishes management's direction that there will be an information security effort and what it is to do. How this is accomplished is defined in security standards.

PROVIDING RESOURCES

At first, basic developmental resources are needed to begin writing information security standards. Later, after standards are published, the required program resources become evident.

What experience and knowledge are required for effective writing of information security policy and standards? The writer should be the person who develops the requirements. A technical writer may be used to polish wording, if appropriate. Helpful background for the writer of a proposal for an information security policy or standard includes the following:

1. Business experience, so that the directives are practical in terms of business goals and operational methods
2. Understanding of the intrinsic value and importance of information in all forms as a competitive business resource
3. A grasp of information systems processes, purposes, and the supporting computer-network infrastructure
4. Understanding of the principles of information security, including access-control methods and administrative and legal processes for all forms of information.

The work of drafting information security policy and standards is not a task for the information systems department. These directives require a broad view of all elements of information in all forms. Security is a management task. Technical competence is useful in some aspects of information security, but initially the writer must understand business operations, risks to information, legal considerations surrounding proprietary claims to information, and the relative values and protection measures described in this book.

Many companies have not developed successful information security programs because the task was assigned to the information systems department, which has only a temporary custodial responsibility for the information asset. The responsibility belongs to the security department, which has expertise in the protection of all forms of information.

A useful approach to gaining participation from the various parties involved, and for ensuring complete coverage, may be found in the three-dimensional matrix described in Chapter 11.

CREATING STANDARDS TO IMPLEMENT INFORMATION SECURITY POLICY

Although initial writing of standards may be assigned by the security director or manager, a number of company functions must review and contribute to the information security standards. Among these are the following:

- Internal auditors
- Functional personnel who are considered information owners, usually the functional managers who budget for or act as primary users of an element of information
- Company staff with special interests in security, for example, finance, personnel, and law
- Information system staff, including those responsible for the most important applications (developers and data center and network operations)

The standards must cover all operational environments in a company. An ad hoc or permanent committee may be helpful for taking responsibility for establishing and maintaining appropriate, timely information security standards.

SUMMARY

Effective information protection requires correct placement of security responsibilities, appropriately defined classification, a useful and flexible directives structure, and a basis in the company's business processes.

NOTES

1.   *ISSA Access*, vol. 3, issue 1, 1990.

14

Administration and Maintenance of Information Security

EMPLOYEE 1: *I think our problems with information security stem from ignorance and apathy.*

EMPLOYEE 2: *Well, I don't know about that, and frankly, I don't care!*

Content is important, but the efficacy of a protection effort depends on continuing administration and maintenance of the information security program. Good maintenance and administration require proper staffing, skills, and organization.

The following are ten minimum requirements:

1. Information security is a critical business task, one that cannot be suitably accomplished as an additional duty imposed on an employee who already has a full-time job. Assignment of information security responsibility as a primary task, to a capable individual, is a prerequisite to success.
2. Information security work is integral with all business activity, and information protection program management must extend across all organizations and through all organizational levels.
3. The skills and technology required for information protection are not the same as the skills and technology for running information systems. Security has a broader context.
4. The scope of information security is business-wide and is not limited to computer or information systems.
5. A good start for information security is not sufficient. Continuing effort, resources, and management attention are required to maintain an acceptable level of protection according to management's risk-acceptance position.
6. The elements of information protection change as business operations and resources change. Continuing analysis is necessary to ensure that security protection meets ongoing business needs. This requirement may well reflect management's willingness to accept greater risk.
7. In a large organization, each unit or group must have an assigned, responsible, and capable information security manager or leader who is empowered to make decisions and commitments on behalf of organization management.

8. The information security manager should report to an executive at the organizational level and in a function that allows freedom of action. This executive, preferably the director of security, should report to a high-level manager, such as an executive vice-president, the general counsel, or the company auditor.
9. Information security must be built into all internal audits.
10. Information security skills include organizational capability, effective personal and group communication, understanding of proprietary legal considerations, a grasp of information systems and computing concepts, a knowledge of good practice in handling, marking, and protecting documents, and a business vision of the information security function.

A detailed discussion of the ten requirements follows. A particular company or industry may have additional needs.

INFORMATION SECURITY REQUIREMENTS

1. Information security is a full-time job.

Information technology and the ways in which information is applied in the business environment are dynamic. That is, information processes—manual and automated—are continuously changing. Provisions for information protection must be designed carefully and evaluated periodically to assure a proper fit. Business management cannot expect a return on a security investment for only one incident.

The employee assigned the task of providing a strategy and program for information protection must see the job as a long-term, permanent position. Job tenure is needed to allow the security manager to become familiar with the subject area. Once a level of expertise is achieved, matters concerning evaluation of program content, security tools and methods selection, and program fine-tuning should present plenty of challenge for even the strongest performer.

In a large organization, one person cannot do the required work. Responsibilities need to be assigned whenever organizational levels or functional differences so justify.

2. Information security work is integral with all business activity.

The fact that there is discussion about security programs probably reflects that business managers do not yet accept security as an integral part of all business activity. Yet managers do consider controls to be essential. No one would think of operating a cost center without financial controls. Yet these are no more important—from a strategic perspective—than information controls. Loss of financial control can affect a company's profits or threaten its success. Similarly, loss or exposure of critical information may destroy a market or product opportunity and could also threaten continued business viability.

An effective information protection program causes every employee to consider information security in all daily activities and decisions concerning creation, distribution, and storage of information. Responsibility for information security must extend across the entire organization, at every reporting level. In some companies employee-awareness programs may be a part-time assignment. In others, proper training of employees and maintenance of a high level of awareness require continuing effort and readily available sources of expertise for all employees who may have questions concerning security procedures.

3.   Information security skills differ from those required to run information systems.

The skills and the body of knowledge required for information security are not perfectly congruent with the skills and knowledge appropriate to information system (computer) work. Computer security is an important part of information security, but not all of it. Information protection requires legal and procedural efforts that are not a part of computer expertise.

Information security experts are needed in the company information systems area. However, broad-based security knowledge that encompasses the legal and procedural aspects (e.g., protection of papers) and computer security principles is necessary to manage a program that protects the company's information rights.

Many senior information system managers now have the title "information manager." This is misleading in most cases because the name implies more than just systems. In practice, however, the job seldom involves the administration of information outside the company's system applications, computers, and networks. Yet, information in paper form is a more severe risk than information in the electronic form.

4.   The scope of information security is business-wide.

Information security is not congruent with *information systems*. Information occurs in many places outside the information system domain. Protection must be provided both inside and outside computer and communications systems. Information protection can never be allowed to be a "systems matter."

5.   Effort must be maintained.

Because information is the core value of any competitive business, its creation, flow, and use tend to change as the business environment, organization, and practices change. No static security effort can keep information secure in a dynamic situation. Knowledgeable people must be continually evaluating security policies and practices to maintain currency with business needs. Program management must be alert and active and must have efficient interfaces with the various operating functions and groups. Periodic use of the three-dimensional matrix (see chapter 11) may be of use in this context.

Periodic meetings of responsible security managers from organizational units within the business with effective planning can produce vital security strategies appropriate to business circumstances and are the basis for continued program vitality.

Unless senior management supports the devotion of personnel resources to the information security effort, security may well founder.

6.   Periodic reviews are essential.

As the business situation or operating environment changes, the information protection effort may have to be redesigned. A protection program out of tune with the rest of the company quickly becomes an anachronism and is disregarded. The managers who approve security standards should be kept appraised of developments in this regard so that modifications to the security standards can be adopted.

7.   Units are responsible for information.

Each unit must have an assigned information security manager or a manager who has information security responsibilities. This manager must be empowered to make information security decisions for his or her organization, after proper consultation.

8.   Information security is important.

The information security manager should report to an appropriate functional executive (e.g., director of audit, director of security, legal counsel) at a high organizational level. This conveys the message that management believes information security to be important.

9.   The audit role is vital.

The company audit department must be an active participant in information security. Audit takes part in the following:

- Defining strategy
- Developing policy statements
- Writing standards in relation to which effective audits may be performed
- Providing trend and risk information essential to maintaining security requirements appropriate to the business situation

10.   Special skills are needed.

Information security is not a job for someone who "has nothing to do." The subject is complex and dynamic. A top performer at an appropriate salary is called for. The information security specialist should understand information technology and use within the business. A more important facility is a grasp of the company's operational processes and a vision of how a particular information protection strategy will fit within those processes. Excellently conceived security measures that are impractical in the business operational environment or that are contrary to company tradition or culture will probably be ineffective at best, and may fail. Simple, modest security requirements that fit with the company's operational methods will probably provide equivalent protection while costing much less, if not in terms of spending, then at least in terms of making the security manager's life more pleasant.

Other skills for the information security specialist may include an understanding of case law in the legal jurisdiction (state or country) involving claims to proprietary information. Most technology companies have had at least one experience in this regard. A primary purpose for information security is to set the groundwork for successfully prosecuting a claim that a piece of information is indeed proprietary. The protective measures established by the information security specialist may well be the determining criteria.

A broad grasp of computer technology and its applications as practiced by the company is important. However, the information security specialist does not necessarily need to be a software whiz or an operating system engineer. In most cases, technical experts in information systems are available for consultation about technical computer security issues. These people often are not the best candidates for information security jobs because they tend to have narrowly focused interests, whereas security risks are broad and varied.

OTHER MAINTENANCE NEEDS

Audit reports and other measurements, such as reports from computer tools on security status in systems, are important input to maintaining management control. Senior executives should demand regular reports on information security status for all business situations throughout the company.

A formal, scheduled review of information security strategies, progress, issues, and proposed solutions should be established. A representative committee empowered to make decisions in a timely manner should be identified. The purpose of this group of managers and specialists concerned with information security is to provide ongoing management of the overall effort. Decisions are based on strategies defined during policy development. This companywide committee (in some companies called the information security committee) provides the midlevel forum in which security issues are distilled before presentation, if necessary, to senior management for decisions or funding. The committee also provides pre-audit early warnings and advice on necessary actions to operating managers. As business changes and new standards become necessary, the committee drives development of the standards and provides a forum for agreement on what is needed.

Figure 14–1 illustrates the organization of information security program maintenance.

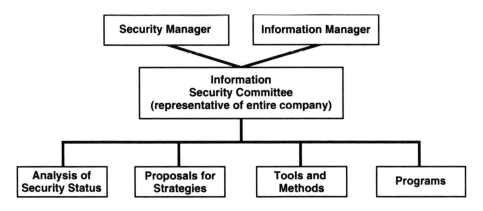

Figure 14–1   Conceptual organization of maintenance.

Glossary with Issues, Concerns, and Solutions

This part of the book presents an alphabetical list of frequently used information security terms. These terms represent common issues that face those concerned with information protection. The suggestions and definitions offered are not all new, nor are they all-inclusive or original to this text. The principles proposed are time tested and practical in most business circumstances.

Access control. Control of physical entry to a facility or object. For information security, the three-step process of authorization, identification, and authentication, which allows a person or process (i.e., a computer program) to have access to information. For mental and written (paper) information forms, access control is authorization to access information based on job assignment and need to know. *Access control* may also refer to the approval required for an authorized person to pass information to another authorized person. For electronic forms of information, control of access to information is accomplished through computer account management and the setting of controls on accounts or files. Such controls might provide for any of a number of options, such as world read, general access, private access, and authorization lists.

Account management. The administrative process that authorizes access to information in computer systems, usually based on assigned job tasks. When job assignments change, the process should promptly remove or modify authorization, for example, when an employee leaves the company or changes jobs. Account management is a record-keeping function closely related to personnel and payroll record-keeping. The computer account management process should be automated in any large business because manual processes require human actions and are unreliable.

Account management (or access and authorization control) is a critical matter. Failure to control computer access is a frequent cause for computer-related crime, fraud, and theft of services.

Account management includes the following:

- Establishing the company's definitions of the types of computer accounts to be allowed. These may include user, group, open, system, courtesy, fixed-function, limited, privileged, and other types.

- Establishing a process for approval or authorization of new accounts and a definition of the justifications therefor. Access is always a privilege related to job assignments and is never a right.
- Establishing a process for creating accounts; involves establishment of computer and manual records related to the user and the user's privileges attached to the account.
- Establishing procedures for periodic account revalidation to ensure that account authorizations are current with business needs and employee job assignments and that accounts are being provided only in line with approval and deletion processes.
- Establishing procedures for the expiration of accounts because of disuse. Accounts that have not been used for long periods of time represent a severe security risk. An unused account may readily fall under the control of someone unauthorized but masquerading as the original, authorized user.
- Establishing procedures for the deletion of accounts when users are transferred, move to a different job, or leave the company. No unnecessary accounts should be in place.
- Determining the company's policy on authorizing accounts for employees who are retired, on disability leave, or on leave of absence.
- Establishing procedures for authorizing and controlling accounts for suppliers, contractors, customers, and other outside parties when business purposes justify their access to company computers.

Administrative security.   Analogous to *account management.* Record-keeping relevant to the authorization of users to access information and the protection of information. May also involve record-keeping essential to physical access control to facilities that are components of the information infrastructure, such as data centers, computer laboratories, communications centers, and copy and facsimile service centers.

In the context of general security, administrative security may include measures such as employee identification badges, incident reporting, investigative reports, facilities control system records, background investigations, and asset-control records. Many of these activities are peripheral to but may have a bearing on information security.

Authenticity.   Proof or demonstration of pedigree; as originally intended; accurate and precise; meeting specifications; representing reality. *Authenticity* means that data are as correct as the user expects them to be, given the subject and the business involved. Authenticity is a characteristic of quality information (see also *information reliability* and *confidentiality.*

Authentication.   Proof of a claim of identity made by a person or a machine to a computer (may be local but usually via networks). Passwords are the most commonly used authentication method but have severe weaknesses. Typical failings in the use of passwords include simple construction leading to easy guessing (*sex* is the most popular password in the United Kingdom according to a survey), lack of confidentiality (many people select an obvious password), and poor use habits (many people share passwords). Computers can generate passwords for users, but this alternative poses other problems involving user acceptance and memory.

Alternatives for authentication include biometric measurements such as hand-prints, voiceprints, fingerprints, and retinal patterns. Also available are supplementary authentication devices, such as smartcards, that contain microcircuits, which interact with the computer and the user to provide strong proof of identity. Cost has deterred general use of these better means of authentication (see also *biometrics*)

Biometrics. Use of unique physical characteristics for personal identification. A simple example is comparison of a picture with the person purportedly shown in the picture. In information security, biometrics is typically used for authentication of an identity claim made to a computer system. Biometric applications use retinal patterns, fingerprints, hand geometry, palm prints, voice patterns, and signature patterns. The authentication system scans the anatomic feature to develop a digital pattern and then compares the pattern with a stored version of the same pattern. To date, such systems have been too expensive to displace the less secure password as the authenticator of choice, except for a few high-security situations. The economics of computing will probably make biometrics more common in the future.

Classification. The basis for all information protection decisions. The process that establishes the sensitivity or value of a particular data element, file, or document. This value or sensitivity level indicates the appropriate effort (investment) to be expended to secure the information. Information that has not been classified is protected or not protected at the judgment of the employee. *Classification* relates to both effectiveness of protection (how well it is done) and efficiency of protection (cost versus benefit).

Information classifications usually are identified by special titles selected for the purpose, such as *Registered Confidential, Restricted Distribution, Private*, or *Personal*. Company information classifications should always be prefixed with the company name to avoid confusion with governmental classification and to ensure proper legal identification, for example, *ABCompany Restricted*. Prudence dictates that businesses avoid classification names used by government entities with which they may deal. In the United States, such terms are *Top Secret, Secret*, and *Confidential*.

Communications security. The devising and application of measures to protect communications circuits and the information traffic thereon. Circuits may include long lines, local networks, radio transmissions, and other methods. All have vulnerabilities. Communications security is closely related to *computer security*. It applies to all types of telecommunications, including data and voice, microwave, satellite, and long line. All networks outside facilities totally controlled by the company must be considered insecure and of high risk (see also *encryption*).

Computer security. The component of information security that deals with the physical and logical protection measures devised and applied to safeguarding computer hardware, software, and operations. Connection of computers to networks markedly increases risk (see also *access control, account management, communications security, information security*).

Computer security software.   See **Software, computer security**.

Computer security tools.   See **Tools, computer security**.

Confidentiality.   The quality of being known only to people or computer processes properly authorized to have access to the information.

Contingency planning.   Planning for a serious emergency or disaster (e.g., flood, fire, loss of power, denial of service). Usually involves back-up and recovery. *Back-up* includes copying and securely storing essential documents, software, and data files, with appropriate periodic refreshment of the stored materials. Back-up may be done electronically and automatically as a part of office routine or data processing, or it may involve manual work and physical transfers. *Recovery* implies some alternative capabilities, including a separate, remote site, available redundant or alternative computers, and redundant or alternative network connections. Uninterruptible power supply is usually a requirement, as are fire alarm and control systems, environmental monitoring systems, and personnel safety systems. All such systems require detailed written procedures and realistic practice sessions at which employees perform the recovery activities. Untried plans are usually only imaginary solutions; even well-tested plans may fail because of unforeseen circumstances.

Case

A company in Europe established a recovery plan that assumed a loss of one of three major data centers. During a test, the team traveled by air to the back-up center only to discover that the operating system software media—kept in a remote vault—had been forgotten.

Digital signature.   The use of encryption processes to assure the recipient of a message that it is genuine and unchanged from the original. Public-key cryptography uses keys in pairs (the sender has a secret key and the addressee has the sender's published public key) and can be used to prevent forgery or disclaimers. The Rivest-Shamir-Adelman (RSA) algorithm is a commonly used method for obtaining digital signatures. The controversial Clipper chip is another method, which involves government access to the secret key for similar purposes.

Disclosure agreement (also called a *nondisclosure agreement*).   A contractual promise by one party to respect the confidentiality of information entrusted to that person by a second party. The receiving party should assign his or her own security classification to the document or computer file to indicate to employees how it is to be handled, even though the originator may have an ownership notice (such as a copyright) or the originator's company classification marked thereon.

Document security.   Protection of information by safeguarding documents. Involves marking, handling, copying, mailing, storing, and destruction controls and procedures. Information on paper constitutes a more serious vulnerability than does electronic information, which can be made more secure on computer media or in storage if properly protected. The plain paper copier and the computer printer are the origins of most sensitive information that finds its way out of the company to competitors or newspapers.

Encryption.   The practical implementation of the science of cryptography. The provision of secrecy by transformation of clear-text information to cipher or unintelligible form by means of processing the data through a mathematical conversion, or algorithm. May be implemented in hardware or software, typically with a key (an alphanumeric set) or large number, which is kept secret. Once encrypted, information cannot be recovered in intelligible (human-readable) form without the key (see also *encryption, public key*)

Encryption, public key.   An asymmetric system in which two keys are used, one for encrypting and another for decrypting. Allows users of the system to publish public keys, which can be used in conjunction with a private or secret key to transform information and to prove origination and integrity of information.

Facility security.   See *physical security.*

Information owner (also called *information sponsor, information manager*).   The business manager responsible for control of a particular information resource or data element. Usually this responsibility is associated with functional authority, e.g., the vice-president of personnel is the information owner of the employee database. The information system department, clerical staff, and security staff may have responsibilities for the personnel data, but these responsibilities are only custodial for a limited purpose. It follows that no one other than the information owner should make classification decisions or determine access authority or privileges for the information owned. Information system staff should never act as information owners.

Information processes.   Manual or automated procedures that generate, process, compile, sort, assemble, edit, audit, test, list, deliver, distribute, and use information (or in its raw, unordered form, data).

Information quality.   Characteristics of good information that are typically the goals of computer and manual system designers and security experts. These characteristics include reliability, integrity, authenticity, and confidentiality. Proper security measures are essential to quality.

Information reliability.   Assurance that quality information is available when and where needed. Implies the protection of the information services infrastructure, including networks, data centers, network switches, offices, libraries, laboratories, and other facilities necessary for the generation and delivery of information at such time and in such places appropriate to business operational requirements. Reliability failures may result from physical, logical, or procedural security problems.

Information security.   The protection of information in all forms. The general forms are written, electronic, and mental. The protection measures devised and applied should be such that the quality of information in any form can be assured. Components of information security are computer security, facility security, communication security, office security, risk management, contingency and recovery planning, and other subjects depending on circumstance and operating environment.

Information security investment.   Justification, approval, or authority necessary to spend money for an identified information security purpose. Information security alternatives can usually be found when purse strings are tight.

Integrity.   The quality of information that implies the information is whole, unimpaired, and unchanged from original; *integrity* may also mean delivered as sent. Integrity in a sense is the responsibility of information system operators, who act as careful custodians of information, although the information system staff should not be information owners.

Logical security.   A division of computer security. Technical, usually nonphysical security measures, including software programs that control or monitor access and privileges, operating system features that separate users and processes, and similar measures. In most companies, a specialized group of technicians manages logical security. Logical security interfaces with administrative security in account management, in which administrative decisions change individual employee access authorizations and privileges typically stored in protected code.

Physical security.   Protective measures used to restrict physical entry to facilities, to protect physical entities (including people), and to protect facilities and their contents from threats of destruction or loss of use. Because the physical (document) form of information poses a serious risk, physical security measures are important in information protection. Physical security elements include but are not limited to closed-circuit television monitors, door locks, guards, controlled-access entryways, fire and burglar alarm systems, and secure storage facilities such as safes or cabinets.

Proprietary rights (also called *proprietary information, trade secrets*).   A potential claim to exclusive possession of and rights to use of specific information. To be able to demonstrate a claim that a piece of information or document is proprietary or a trade secret, the business must show that the particular information in question has been identified (typically by classification of the information) as having unique value or sensitivity, that the company has established procedures to protect the information, and that the company's employees routinely follow protection procedures in the course of normal business operation. Many plaintiffs seeking to prove proprietary rights have foundered on this last requirement (see also *supplementary information security measures*)

Reliability.   See *information reliability.*

Risk management (also called *risk analysis, risk assessment*).   Study of the threats and vulnerabilities associated with an activity or course of action. In information security, usually an examination of an information application or procedure to determine the value of the risks being taken (e.g., monetary exposure), to determine proper protective measures, and to evaluate the risk-to-benefit ratio of the costs of such measures. Many computer software packages are available to assist in such analysis. In general, the process consists of identifying risks, assigning a probability and cost to each risk, multiplying the cost by the probability to arrive at a ranking, and using the ranking to determine security investment priorities. Most risk assessments are based on estimates or are the product of a multiplication of estimates.

Risk assessment is most effective when limited to a single application or situation. Company-wide risk assessment suffers from the inevitable ongoing changes in the business environment, the compounding of estimates during the process, and the dynamics of business strategies and processes. The resulting risk data are usually suspect and expensive.

Smartcard.   A plastic card (similar to a credit card) with integrated circuitry, including read only memory (ROM), that contains authentication data. Cryptographically encoded identity numbers and time-generated codes may be used with or without direct interface to computer systems. Typically used in conjunction with passwords or other user interactions to authenticate a user to a computer system.

Software, computer security.   Packages of programs that allow a business to manage and control access to computer resources. IBM's RACF and Computer Associates' CA-ACF2 are examples. Modern security packages allow decentralized control of mixed computer platforms, which are essential to an organization that uses various interconnected computer brands and that has thousands of authorized employees, perhaps spread worldwide (see also *access control* and *account management*).

Supplementary information security measures.   Legal measures such as copyrights and patents. Legal precautions may help assure ownership rights but have little to do with confidentiality, which is often a prerequisite to a legal claim to ownership. In some cases, information may be both copyrighted and company classified. However, copyrighted information may be publicly disclosed, so a copyright is not the equivalent of classification if confidentiality is the purpose of the action. All patents are publicly disclosed in the patent process, but they assure a period of exclusive rights to the patent owner.

Tools, computer security.   Hardware or software mechanisms that provide or support necessary computer or network security functions. For example, security tools may support information classification labeling on computer file headers or print files, account management, confidentiality of storage and transmission, security violation detection and countermeasures (this is typically an artificial intelligence application), enforcement of and provision for individual user accountability, message and network node authentication, and security violation management including investigative support. Tools may be active in that the tool searches or monitors and responds, as opposed to many security software systems that are passive in that the user must take action to derive benefit. Digital Equipment Corporation's INSPECT product is illustrative of a security status enforcement and reporting tool.

Trade secret (also called *proprietary information*).   Information that is closely held, that is, controlled and not generally known, even within the company, and has commercial value, that is, it contributes in an essential way to profitability. As defined under *information security*, companies must establish effective programs for information protection if they wish to establish their proprietary (or trade secret) rights.

Index